Scrapbo

By Coleman Barks

Coleman Barks

Scrapwood Man

POETRY AND PROSE

7/8/07

For Paul,
and with gratitude
for his work.

Coleman Barks

Maypop
ATHENS, GEORGIA

Maypop Books
196 Westview Dr.
Athens, GA 30606

800-682-8637

colemanbarks.com

ISBN 1-884237-04-5

Some of these were previously published in the following: *Atlanta Quarterly, Tiferet, Figdust, Parabola,* and *Seneca Review.*

Emily Dickinson's poem #520 is published by permission of Harvard University Press.

The cover images are from photographs taken by Benjamin Barks of pieces of heartpine from The Beauty Parlor, 1918 West Broad, Athens, Georgia.

for Ed Hicks

Table of Contents

LOSING IT

Guidance We Have Need Of

. . . in winter enjoy.
—Blake

Late winter afternoon sliding by in silence. This delight of reading
Bill Merwin's *Purgatorio*, the notes especially. The text being
sometimes so settled in the politics of Dante's Florence I lose
interest. I find a mistake. A note for Canto X should read *2nd
Samuel,* not *2nd Kings.* The passage when David dances before the
ark. Dante says that David's dancing makes him both less and more
than a king, a condition we have no single word for, the fool in his
glory.

I was given a word in a dream recently, *frontiseratory.* I move to a
dictionary, then know something else for sure, that I can be given a
word in a dream, but I cannot look it up. Though I can and do when
I wake, in a Latin glossary. *Frontis,* the face, the forehead, the
emblem across from the title page, what is apparent to others that I
cannot see, what I can know with blunt fingers. This naked device,
this guidon I carry through town to draw sidewards across a pillow.

There is a lot of attention to face and forehead in the *Purgatorio,*
the most beautiful being at the end of Canto I when Virgil spreads
out his hands and lays them on the grass that is soaked wet with
dew. Dante sees what his friend is about and leans his face near to
let Virgil wash the tear stains and restore the color which their
journey through hell has drained. I want a friend like Virgil to wash
and restore my face with hands dipped in cold sopping fresh dew. I
have had in the past such friendship walking with me through the
smoke. Now pure absence looms like wisdom that wears this form
out as it tries to find and give others these ablutions.

Let the reader make now the familiar two-handed gesture of wiping
his or her face in a cleansing release from wherever we just were—
near-sleep, prayer, reading, the leaning-back of a winter afternoon.
So this then is purgatory, where we finally weep to be purified and
begin to become the empty expanse we see is next.

Reading in Bed

Looking for the phrase *egotistical sublime*
in Keats' letters, hoping for a new way
to attack myself. He was giving a slap
to Wordsworth's verbosity, which I accept
as my own, deciding every time now
I am in a bookstore, I'll carry home a poet
I ought to know well but don't. Marianne Moore,
Robinson Jeffers. Lord Weary. The mind *is*
an enchanting thing.
               Rabindranath Tagore
would go off by himself for months
to a houseboat in Kashmir to read and write.
One night reading Benedetto Croce by candle,
he blew out the flame and lay there
letting his eyes get used to the dark,
and the full moon's other kind of light
magnified by its sublimation on lakewater
rose around him in bed like the extinguished mind.

Notebooks

At a Sunday night supper, September 28th, 1890, Whitman is talking with friends. He pauses with a piece of chicken on his fork suspended between the four of them around a square table.

> *Leaves of Grass* can never be understood except by indirection. Pauses again. It stands first for that something back of phenomena, in phenomena, which gives it all its significance, yet cannot be described —which eludes definition, yet is the most real thing of all.

He puts the bite in his mouth and chews and moves to another subject. Horace Traubel was one of those there, and the notes he took on the times he spent with Whitman during Whitman's last year are published in a number of volumes called *With Walt Whitman in Camden*.

I am reading this remembered bit of monologue in a cafeteria booth when a black man about my age, late 60s, walks by and stops, looking down at my plate of chicken bones. That chicken been on hard times. He waits for my response to this generosity. I say, Yeah. He's bout had all the fun he's going to have.

He turns and goes, laughing. I love that human trait of turning and laughing, then walking away without further verbal reply, implying that's all this moment needs.

****

Early spring twilight in Oxford, England, March 12, 1870. Gerard Manley Hopkins writes in his journal outdoors as this is happening.

> A fine sunset: the higher sky dead clear blue bridged by a broad slant causeway rising from right to left of wisped or grass cloud, the wisps lying across; the sundown yellow. Moist with light but ending at the top in a foam of delicate white pearling and spotted with big tufts of cloud in colour russet between brown and purple edged with brassy light.

> But what I note it all for is this: before I have always taken the sunset and the sun as quite out of gauge with each other, as indeed physically they are, for the eye after looking at the sun is

blunted to everything else, and if you look at the rest of the sunset, you must cover the sun, but today I *inscaped* them together and made the sun the true eye and ace of the whole, as it is.

It was all active and tossing out light and started as strongly forward from the field as a long stone or a boss in the knop of a chalice stem; it is indeed by stalling it so that it falls into the scape of the sky.

I look up *knop*. The round raised place
at the bottom of the center of the inside
of the cup used for the sacrament.

One might notice it
as one drank the chalice wine,
the node draining red.

He stalls the sun to let it be a boss,
the ace that makes his hand,
starting forward like a fallen plinth.

I bow to the beauty of a childhood
no-leaf brackenlight riversheen spring.

Next morning.

A heavy fall of snow tufted and toed the firs and yews and went on until they were taxed beyond their spring. The limes, elms, and turkey-oaks it crisped as with young leaf.

Looking at the elms from underneath you see every wave in every twig become by this the wire-like stem to a finger of snow, and to the hangers and flying sprays it restores to the eye the inscapes they had lost beautifully brought out against the sky, which is on one side dead blue, on the other washed with gold.

Inscape, keeness that inhabits light,
the 'scape inward.

****

A Friday in January, 1891, Traubel stops in to see Whitman "at 5:48 pm." He tells about some article he has read on *spirituality*. Whitman looks at him.

That depends entirely on what a man means by *spirituality*. Here is a world of individuals, each with some fresh, peculiar, demonstration of it. I throw myself back on Elias Hicks in all matters of this kind. Elias would say we are all spiritual, by the very necessities of our natures, every man in his measure. We can no more escape it than the hearts that beat in our bosoms. I haven't the least doubt that here he touched bottom. Think of Bob: the grand glorious justification of Bob is that from head to foot *he is flushed with the square*—every line of him—of his books—bathed in justice, love of right, human generosity, to a degree I fail to find in any other.

Three days later.

I read to Whitman from the *Bulletin* how an Australian playbill announces among its attractions, "Walt Whitman's Whimsical Wheezes." A San Francisco newspaper wants to know when the good grey poet went into the business.

Horace reports Whitman had a good, long laugh over this. The playwrighting *business* I guess they mean, or the whimsical wheezing trade of freeverse poetry. Accumulating playful breath-units, not bad.

Whitman heard the Quaker *inner light* preacher, Elias Hicks, when he was ten, and took from that a *natural* kind of oratory. Part Indian, part black, Hicks put a powerful simpleness in Whitman's flow. Tenderness and strong resolve blending. Later in a biographical sketch of Hicks, Whitman admires in the man's speaking a human magnetism that rowsed rapport and intuition in those who listened deeply.

Whitman's motto above his writing table was: *Make the Works.* He died March 26, 1892. At the funeral four days later passages were read from Confucius, Buddha, Plato, the Qur'an, the Bible, and *Leaves of Grass*.

The Bob above, agnostic Colonel Ingersoll, said at the service, Death is less terrible than it was before. Thousands and millions will walk into the dark valley of the shadow holding Walt Whitman by the hand.

****

From Tolstoy's *Last Diaries,* 1910, the final year of his life. He was eighty-one.

> Jan. 25th—After three, am going walking. I feel well in my soul, but I am repellent to myself and glad of it.

He wonders greatly about his identity.

> Feb. 13th—What is this thing which is conscious? I do not know and cannot know. There is no I. There is only what is in me.

He walks, or rides horseback almost every day, answers six to ten letters, frets about sick relatives, works on articles, a piece on suicide, stories, but is rarely pleased with what he has done. He is very much in the present and also feeling strongly another reality that he might waken into.

> March 2nd—Am going to bed. Dinner, chess, gossip, cards, gramaphone, and I felt painfully ashamed. I shall not participate more. I shall read.

He has nine months to live.

Wine Poems

The short poems of a man drinking wine
are considered moving if the poet is Chinese
and out in a boat after midnight twelve hundred years ago,
and they are. It is wonderful we have any record
of the moment of a tipsy man named Po Chu-i
reading poetry in a boat by lamplight.

I pick up your scroll of poems and read one aloud.
The poem ends, the lamp gutters, sky not yet light.

My eyes hurt. I put out the lamp and go on sitting
in the dark: the sound of the waves blown by headwinds
sloshing against the boat.

Yuan was the friend he was reading, as I am,
sitting in my study after three a.m.
drinking an Australian merlot,
as someone else will be in 3181, listening

to the heartbreaking friendship of poets,
unless by then we have managed to snuff out
the joy of floating and hearing a poem
making its unique sound against the boat
under the half-lit sky before dawn.

If I don't do Zen meditation to wipe out deluded thoughts
then I must pace around drunkenly, spouting crazy songs.

Otherwise in the autumn moon, or with these evenings
of spring breeze, how am I to bear the idle
longing for the past that comes through me?

That's Po Chu-i "Forcing Myself
to Drink." I could read another called
"Tied up for the Night in a Cove,"
but I'll put a cork on it and go upstairs
to sleep with the tao of poetry under my bed-boat.

The Vivaldi Brothers

Two Genovese brothers named Vivaldi sailed through the Straits of
Gibralter in 1291. They had already explored the west African coast.
This time they sail out of sight due west from Morocco, never to be
seen again. So now there is a Vivaldi Brothers holiday, the first
Monday in March, diametrically opposed on the calendar to
Columbus Day, first Monday in October. It is when we celebrate the
two extra blessed centuries that the elegant, intuitive native
civilizations of North and South America were spared from the
monsters taking shape in the minds of European empire-builders,
Protestant purists, and gold-mad Spanish horse-enthusiasts. They
continue for two hundred and one dreamtime years to bake pots
and weave exquisite fabric, not to mention perform blood sacrifice
with their young people. But they are mostly gentle in their spirit-
yearning. They go on retreat to high mountains and draw shamanic
rock art visions that come to them. Some even record a spooky
longterm prediction that takes into account our disasterous
interruption of their art, their ways of knowing and seeing mystery.

Plantsongs

To some it is given to hear the singing of plants, as well as that of the birds. Such a lucky one in his or her solitary walking over the fields, takes the plantsongs in, and the power of eloquence increases, so sharpening and cleansing sight that as such a one comes back to the house, the walls and roof have grown transparent. There is no indoor-outdoor distinction anymore, yet he, or she, is still warmed, protected from weather, and afforded privacy from ill-meaning wanderers.

Verses for Children to Memorize

II Kings 2:23-25. And he went up from thence unto Bethel: and as he was going by that way, there came forth little children out of the city and mocked him, and said unto him, Go up, thou bald head; go up, thou bald head. And he turned back, and looked on them, and cursed them in the name of the Lord. And there came forth two she-bears out of the wood, and tare forty and two of them. And he went forth from thence to Mount Carmel and from thence to Samaria.

But the story of the she-bears and the torn-up forty-two children followed Elisha even unto Jericho and it was known by this that he did not like the children to mock and call attention to his hairloss.

The Speed of Consciousness and August 18th

In a restaurant near Peggy's Cove, Nova Scotia, an old man takes
tiny stroke-steps going table to table. Watch out for that saw. It'll
cut your head off. The crosscut blade on the wall above my head, a
lumbering theme. Next table. Did you quit drinking yet. A man
says, I know you. Twenty years ago in Colorado you had a boat
rental place. I did. Small world. Where do you live now? Where do I
live now. I don't know. Everyone laughs. The two women he's with,
equally as old, come out of the restroom. It's still the same day, he
says. Where do we live? Fort Payne. Twenty years. I didn't recognize
you with your teeth in. He shuffles out having held highspirited,
clairvoyant conversation with all in the dining area. Now he shows
us how to exit, jimdandy in the midst of menace. The three take
their eternity to get to the car, then the getting in, and the floating
slowly from the parking lot. He waves from the backseat like a baby,
like a king in exile, like the founder of a myth re-enactment pageant
inside the iron turtle of enough time.

Latin and an Almost Extinct Songbird

I have a diorama in my study that you can look into and see an old
afternoon, a villa out in the country near Rome, in the first century.
Virgil is walking a colonnade at the edge of a garden; there is a
slight breeze. If you put your ear to the see-through hole, you can
hear him say the lines he is working on in Book VI.

> *facilis descensus Averno . . . .*
> *sed revocare gradum suprasque evader ad auras,*
> *hoc opus, hic labor est.*

The descent to hell is easy, but to make
one's way back, to retrace the steps
up out into the golden air, that
is difficult, and this is the work.

What he says is a central human truth, built into everyone. We
descend the pit of unconsciousness in different ways, at varying
speeds. Aggression, jealousy, coldness, addiction, fear, rage,
compulsive sensuality, pretended elation, denial, hypocrisy. No one
can tell us how or when to stop the descent and begin a return,
composing the way that lifts into late afternoon light, tender and
ruined and still.

I am driving around this windy Friday in March as though a
renovated suburb were my psyche, the duration I explore, what I
was told early to glorify and enjoy, shriven along a flickering street
in the reprieve of light.

> *. . . evader ad auras . . .*

emerging to brightness

> *. . . hoc opus, hic labor est . . .*

this being the work and how it gets done.

The wonder through the keyhole is hearing seagulls and a European
songbird, the softgrey turtledove with goldgreen eyes, almost
extinct, found only on the Isle of Man, and gliding the gilded air of
Virgil's verse.

The world that leaves, taking some of this one with it, can be heard
better than it can be seen. We go with it into demolition, returning
as residue, a lightness, and not much else.

Watertrance

I think only of James Agee, but I am sure that several American writers have written about their fathers watering lawns at twilight, how they would hold the hose and use a thumb to spray various arcing fans, and do that long into the dark, well after sprinklers were invented. We love the sweet relaxing of our fathers into watertrance. Mine was an administrator for forty-five years at a boys' boarding school, with all that talking to parents and listening to teacher squabbles, evenhandedly not taking sides, staying aloof from friendship with the teachers, and facing directly the final violence of *shipping* a boy. That was the word for packing him home permanently for doing something spectacularly bad like sneaking out at night, commandeering the school bus that the keys were always in to go downtown and drink beer at Bob Green's. Dad hid his drinking mostly, except at the country club. We knew he had whisky bottles behind the towels in the little bathroom, but no one mentioned it. I would look in there every few months, different bottles, different liquid levels. He was never drunk that I knew about, sometimes more extraverted, more curious and talkative, though never slurred or unsteady. Sometimes he got a bad headache in the afternoon that I would go down to the infirmary and get him empirin for. That was the drinking. He would ask me to give him a massage with rubbing alcohol. I felt privileged to bear down on his powerful shoulder muscles. *That feels good,* he'd say. He was very faithful about watering the boxwood, August evenings pulling the hose around to every plant, giving each a thirty-minute soak of his ancient patience, under the dry rising-fall of cicadas, complaining their rejoicing. Now I hear, and *see,* (in dream) my father's footsteps coming in the front hall, the clear movement of his shoes walking relaxed there, home again. He sympathizes with me that I have inherited his *damnable* love of drinking. There are two other adjectives he uses that I cannot remember. I'll make them up. His and my *boxwooden, august* thirst for bourbon.

Gurdjieff's Teaching

In the fall of 1925 when Gurdjieff was about to leave France to spend the winter in New York, he called a meeting of those who would remain behind to explain their work assignments. Miss Madison, who was to direct the activities of the school, served tea. She has an unusual way of doing it. Standing at the tea table, she pours a cup and then brings it to where each person is seated. As she stoops, bending from the waist, she delicately passes wind in a small refined report, from which unembarrassed she straightens, says pardon me, and returns to the table. This continues with each delivery. From the edge of the circle Gurdjieff supplies commentary. Miss Madison has special qualities not immediately apparent. Her exceptional manner of serving tea for example, the slight bow to each recipient, accompanied by the sound of a toy gun and the instantaneous politeness of her apology, gives her a graciousness that is unique. As Gurdijeff continues at flowery length on this soft zen cannonade of a tea ceremony, Miss Madison keeps flawless composure. The end result is a strengthening of her directorship. There are many reasons to love Miss Madison, but Gurdjieff's focus on her endearing, superbly bland victory over bodily shame makes her command in his absence profound, particularly when she asks someone in the group for a report.

Bardic Schools

On the island of Barra, at the southern tip of the Outer Hebrides, for the final stage in the training of a poet, a round stone hut is built with an entrance in the top. No windows. The novitiate enters and lies down. The master places a stone on his chest and closes him in the hut for three days. The idea of the stone on the chest is to make him more conscious of breathing, the rhythm and irregularities, so that his thinking and breathing grow congruent with the language being assembled. Robert Hass says poetry is breath-sculpture. In the bardic schools poetry sprang from remembering breath in the dark. After three days of fasting and seclusion you are expected to recite three new poems. The immuring presumably puts you in a timeless place like the one where God was before the thought of light. The poignancy of imagery, the bits of it brought to mind with words, is heightened in the sensory deprivation. Spirit-pressure increases, and that is the source of our best creating. No one knows really how language craft occurs. In another account of the practice each poet before he goes to sleep chooses a subject from a list of possible ones, and then retires to a hut. The next morning one eats very little and stays inside the private enclosure all day, mostly lying on a cot with a plaid cloth over his eyes. In the evening each is given pen and paper to write down what he has made, and later that night each poet performs a new poem for the group. Then they eat and drink, engage in lively conversation, and are given the next subject, sustaining this level of work for nine days. Do we lack opportunity, or discipline, in our chaotically diverse lives for such devotion to word-work? If I were to experiment, I would choose a high desert plain with huts situated a mile from each other. Taking notes will be allowed, on handmade paper with pens equally magnificent. The night performance hall is handcrafted carpentry. Every poet has the entire range of world-class musicians to choose from and state-of-the-art audio-visuals, whatever they want. A small library of two shelves is allowed in the retreat, along with a reading chair, a lamp, bed and full bath. No computers or phones, no television or radio, no recorded music. I may relent on the music. The information on what happened in the bardic schools comes down through the oral tradition and from the Marquis de Clanricarde's *Memoirs* published in 1722. He visited a school in the Outer Hebrides in the late 17th Century. His notes are thought to be reliable. I have recently begun a practice that fits in with such a school of poetics. At some point during the day—it has been around 7:30 pm recently—I light a candle and play Stephen Mitchell's cassette of him reading one of the Duino Elegies. I follow with the text open on the kitchen table. I listen to only one poem, making notes of what strikes me, replaying parts, or the whole thing. Today was the Third. Rilke's Duino Elegies and the Sonnets to Orpheus, those quick tufts that sprout between the larger terraces, present as vast and subtle a model as we have of soul-consciousness. Macchu Picchu is the scene I see. It is all soul-identity. Let's say we have this personality that continues to take shape, more or less crystallized, more or less quirky, brilliant, dull. Coleman, Andrew, Ann, Robert, Nils, Ivana, Lou. But we are also a mystery that is not pronominal, has no persona. It is that field that writes The Duino Elegies and the Sonnets to Orpheus, that are so full of unanswerable questions, the real ones, *Who am I?* being foremost. And how do I sustain friendship with those elusive beings, the ones that Rilke calls *angels*. In the Third Elegy there are presences, one a comfort, a hush, a mothering. The other is a rivergod of the blood, a passionate male wanting to break open the abyss of his desire, to shred himself and begin again. Those two opposed figures sit across from each other and have been simmering inside me since I was seven. Less confrontive, now the sexual surface is smoothing. My friend John Seawright drove to Atlanta in the mid-1970s to see a Patti Smith concert. Somehow he gets back to her dressing room at intermission. I have something for you, he says, handing her his copy of the *Duino Elegies*, Stephen Spender's translation. I have three copies of this at home, she says. After intermission she reads sections from it to the crowd, and tearing out each page as she finishes, she floats them over the audience like ash.

Glee and Other Substances

Inexplicable moments do occur. One Saturday morning a few years ago my sister Betsy woke with blood on each wrist, about a quarter of a cup total, her estimate, sticky, bright red. There were no cuts, and it was not menstrual blood. Her hawk-minded, no-nonsense husband saw the same sight. Maybe it's one of those Jesus things, says Mike. A *stigmata*, Betsy howls. They change the sheets and go about their sweet Saturday ritual, coffee in Concord, walking. The Monday afterward a woman calls Mike in his Boston office at *The Atlantic*. As an aside she tells him to remind Betsy of when they saw blood on Doctorow's wrists. Betsy has no memory of the woman or of seeing blood on the novelist's wrists. I wish they had kept a smear sample. Whose blood was that? I feel that enlightened souls like Jesus, Francis, Ramana, Meher Baba, Rinzai, Rabia, Shams, Bawa Muhaiyaddeen, Rumi, those bright fields of awareness, continue after death to work within those who love them. Blood with no wound might be a message of some kind for Betsy to decipher. A conversation with Jesus. My teacher died on December 8th, 1986. In the late 80s he came to me in a dream with gifts, jewel shards in a compartmented box, and a jar of balsam. I accidentally turned the jar over, but it did not spill. I righted the jar, no harm done. Where did you get this, I ask. He laughs and says, *1369 Gregory*. I look on maps and question people. Then it occurs it might mean 1369 on the Gregorian calendar, which turns out to be both the year the Kashmiri poet, Lalla, met her Sufi teacher, Ali Hamadani, and the year Hafez collected his poems into a volume. I have felt drawn to work on these two poets, and I accept the connection, as well as the one with Rumi, as gifts from Muhaiyaddeen, revealer of light, *givens* I have done nothing to deserve. I was talking with another Sufi, Babasahib from Karachi, telling him the dream. When I get to the point where I tip over the balsam, he interrupts, *But it did not spill.* Anyone who knows the consistency of balsam, of course, knows it would take hours for the thick substance to flow out. Balsam. Visionary moments happen, as does conversation with whatever one calls the presence we inhabit, a consciousness living well beyond the personality's limits. For me that is the most exciting human experience. Any science of the psyche must include some acknowledgement of those exchanges.

In high school I was in the Glee Club, which was four rows of ten guys standing on risers in the front of the chapel singing Old Mahn River, Stouthearted Men, There is Nuthin like a Dame, with always the finale, The Battle Hymn of the Republic. In the beauty of the lilies Christ was borne across the sea with a glory in his bosom that transfigures you and me. Such lush seraphic sentences we sang those Thursday nights of glee. I recall how walking home one night my voice was a dark petal-flame over the river, wild indigo and gold. We see the mystery clearer as we grow older, which is some balm against the disappointment of losing mobility.

Car Trips

In the late 1940s my father took me along on his summer trips to various headmaster association meetings in New England, he and I driving north through Knoxville and Kingsport, Roanoke, Washington, New York, Hartford. I loved maps. I was nine, ten, eleven. Surely he would rather have gone on those trips alone, but it was part of the psychology strategies recommended to my parents, I found out later, to help me get over my stammering, which back then and maybe now too, was thought to be connected with Oedipus. Having too easily won my mother in the family drama, I unconsciously feared my father's anger, and that nervous tension stuck in my throat, strangling language, the theory goes. On those long summer drives he and I got to be traveling buddies, his hat on the back of his head, taking it easy. I would wander whatever campus we were on, exploring, like Trinity Univesity in Hartford. I grew up on a campus and have always felt at home in the gothic archways and amongst the boxwood of campi. Or he would put me on a tour bus or a boat around Manhattan, and get some couple to keep an eye on me. I loved the whole thing, the Smithsonian, god, I could have lived in there. The old blacktop roads led out of Chattanooga on the way to seeing the world with my dad, looking down at the map, then up at the skyline of New York across tall mudflat cattails. Neither of us knew then or now what the other was carrying, guilt, ecstasy, humiliation, glory, impotence, his terror at the sight of his brother Charles' ears and nose exploding in stroke-blood, coming up the stairs toward him. I love my father and the way he took me with him, so I could soak up who he was and how well he meant by me, the two of us sitting together on the front seat day after August day in what is surely one of the *true* ways we have to help each other. What we talk about is hardly it. This good deep silence shared in the sympathetic hum of our spinal columns. I still feel his quietness nearby, dead since 1971, his half-smile, the cigar smoke. *Hey bud.*

The Return of Professor Dumwhistle

Mr. Penny sat me on a big dining hall table carried outdoors under the three hundred year old oak tree in front of forty playcampers aged four to six. I was nine. This was summer, 1946. I had gone behind the green storage cabinet and put on the fake nose-glasses-eyebrows he had gotten somewhere and a tall hat. He introduces me as Professor Dumwhistle, who can answer any question. And I do, suddenly much goofier and more confident, wilder than any way I have ever been in my short, shy, hesitant, stammering life. I did not recognize it then, but it was a ploy, part of a number of tremendously sweet efforts that my parents and others on top of that hill made, to help me break through my speech difficulties. None of them worked, not the stammering pills, not the hypnosis by Dr. Polgar, not the black butterfly inkblotches, nothing loosened my spring-source, my sounding out into this melodious, commodious, ventricular vehicle, this burble of rivering grace conducted over the earth by multiple amplification systems, this bass viol of tenderness and pretension. Nothing did any good, until sex took hold and gave me tongue. When I began to swim naked at night with naked girls my age, a luminous chrisming coal, a moon, a nude synonym, a ruby-lit grape, a berry on its waggly stem, touched and opened my mouth to flame, a wand within a cone, a ridged hallway to the other world. Dumwhistle is no longer a professor, though at seventy we hear he is active in retirement, a moderately well-known minor poet, traveling mystic, out-of-body facilitator, party guest, sufferable clairvoyant, and occasional sperm donor.

(bird whistling)

Dumwhistle's whistle is no longer dumb. His unruly eyebrows have become real. They zigzag out of his very brain. He walks on top of speckled daylight on the ground like a medium-size bird. He has no tableseat of crazy wisdom, no answers, and he wears no hat.

Purring

The internet says science is not sure
how cats purr, probably
a vibration of the whole larynx,
unlike what we do when we talk.

Less likely, a blood vessel
moving across the chest wall.

As a child I tried to make every cat I met
purr. That was one of the early miracles,
the stroking to perfection.

Here's something I've never heard:
a feline purrs in two conditions,
when deeply content and when
mortally wounded, to calm themselves,
readying for the death-opening.

The low frequency evidently helps
to strengthen bones and heal
damaged organs.

Say poetry is a human purr,
vessel mooring in the chest,
a closed-mouth refuge, the feel
of a glide through dying: one

winter morning on a sunny chair
inside this only body, a far-off
inboard motorboat sings
the empty room, urrrrrrrrrrrrhhhhhhhhh
             urrrrrrrrrrrrhhhhhhhhh
             urrrrrrrrrrrrrhhhhhhhhhh

A Note to Purring

Now a woman comes to tell me
her cat purred all through giving birth
to eleven kittens, oiling the door
for those already begun within the womb
to purr for having to die

and for the ecstatic uhnnnn of winter
solitude, and to practice
for how they will later sing their own
young loose to crossover air
with chthonic, bassal surf,
so distinct from any screek-yowl
of gull or tom.

We do not know how we manage
to combine the umbilical voice
with this ventriloqual trickery,
ignorance being in the mix
and no hindrance for the mothering
push of breath and uhnn to word.

These Winter Skies

Once in the middle of love for a woman. She is going away for three months, telling me not to worry. I am weeping, waiting for her to come back from the city where she is a lover of another, with her fidelity to two, country mouse and city mouse. I do not want to be a hermit, though I do want more moments of clear perception that living alone brings. She says there is no way to control any of this. We lie down with our shoes off. This is the way we clean house, inside a fierce, changing music. I am growing old and still delight to learn something out of an encyclopedia. I have a confused heart and no set aesthetic. There are dances I have never tried, lounging in a scrounge of watchfulness, with no private life, more a mid-region like a theatre auditorium or a restaurant, where I perform in the aisles and then the parking lot. These winter skies, I can almost imagine living with one of them, inside the buckling we call *kneeling*, with evening birdbits distributing themselves. Seedsound in a cold diamond, the superb ache when a few hours of writing begin.

I would like to hear what you have escaped, how you slipped free from some compulsion or inherited conditioning. What moves your story along? Tangents, errands, resupply. Desire, absence of desire, partial fulfillment. Galway says that, at seventy-seven, desire is still to him the most beautiful thing. I would rather some fluency come, usefulness and a longed-for spontaneity. Robert Graves to the very end was writing love poems for his muses, women with muse-potential, always on the lookout for new ones. I have heard people dismiss those late love poems as silly, not appropriate for the elder, the great shaman. But it is those poems that feel most alive to me, unburdened by thought, so lightly set loose, a tissue, barely there.

Spirit and a Fall Night

A small piece of notepaper with a rusted paperclip mark, from a Friday night open reading in Passaic, NJ, in the late 1970s. I remember passing through Passaic, but not making this list.

> an excon in tennis shoes and bluejean jacket singing high with his eyes shut
>
> a black man doing an experimental hopping poem (I spell it *hoping*. Maybe it was hoping.)
>
> big guy, old, with children's poetry from a Montana reservation
>
> plaid shirt pro, with a new Wasteland including something—I can't be sure of the word—It looks like *ratios*.

There is a mysticism of watching and listening to each other, no matter our mammoth ignorance of its workings. A community room, metal chairs, a fall night. Rudolf Steiner says there is an activity inside human thinking, and that impulse to move and make is spirit. To sing before a group, to close your eyes as song comes over, to watch what goes on between us as it happens. Is this attention and that relaxing what Steiner calls the *activity inside thinking?*

Good as Dead

With my deli sandwich I sometimes sit
under a big poster of B.B.King,
eyes almost closed, cheek resting on his hands
folded over the headstock where the tuning pegs are.

There is a rectangular jeweled shield
on the left ring finger and a prongheld bezel
on his left little.

The guitar neck inlaid with mother-of-pearl
says *Lucille*, the woman who calls in
ocean detail for the turtleskin back of his hands.

Strong silver steel strings stretch down
and off the bottom waiting to be told,
BE BE

We wait as music make us wait,
as good as dead. Hello honeypot.

My friend Seawright comes in dream
to a live friend Debi to tell her
to tell me he's fine; *happy*
the word used, which when living
I never knew him to.

She leaves the message on my machine.
Surely the here and gone converse.

Listen to the clock of this fire-ticking woodpop
white pine. Two old women,
Miss Rhodes and Miss Williams,
brought three trees from North Carolina
that Henry Girard has now cut down
and rather than haul away,
two men split and stack
for me for fifty dollars.

This is the material plane where logrings
spun into smoke get paid for
with wordpaper tossed in. I have heard
the Buddha was sitting with a group near the end

of his life. He said you may ask me anything,
except there must be nothing about God,
the soul, liberation, death, love, the transmission
of light, peace, desire, the mystery of the blessed one,
suffering, enlightenment, or what it means
to die before you die.

I pick a redstripe cigar wrapping-opener
from the step in front of me. Nearly napping,
I am sweeping the twelve backstairs
with an image behind the sunlight delighting
my eyes, of a woman with bare breasts,
white silk sliding across.

Shovel Throw

The town is gathering for the event.
First up, a likely specimen,
thirty-seven, thereabouts, in the stronger sinew
that comes just past athletic prime.

Lets go, fifty-eight yards.
He'll get a few more. What kind of work
do you do? I'm a farmer. Nod.

Second. Late twenties, the peak.
Throws it sixty-one yards. What occupation?
Construction. Ahh.

Now comes we're not sure what. No tone,
no bone, no beef, a little smiling runt.
Slings it seventy-seven yards, not a bother.

Excuse me, sir, we have to know.
What kind of job do you hold?

When I was ten years old, my father and I
were walking. There was a shovel
leaning against a shed.

Do you know what that is, son? A shovel.
My advice to you is, whenever you see one of those things,
take and throw it as far as you can.
I have never done a day's work in my life.

The story comes across from Ireland,
from the peat bogs, as do I.

Some distant kin has done research
on the BARKS coat-of-arms. The usual rigamarole
on a shield, but with a shovel *rampant*.

An Armand Hammer Baking Soda arm cocked
holding a shovel. So the call for me is double.

Down into the dirt, scrabbling chirt-scrape,
then the resting lull,
leaning-talkatoo and lookabout I have been at
since I first held round wood.

But also *up*.
The zing-zing-zing overhead of a shovel
winging like a freed propeller.

Band Concert

Clarke Middle School gymnasium with coolish spring light coming through the upper wire-mesh window glass, May 13, 2003, 7 pm. It is the band concert that everybody plays in. The seventh grade first: the best of Beethoven, It Don't Mean a Thing, and Sing, Sing, Sing, which I remember dancing the shag to in another gymnasium.

The sixth grade is next. My granddaughter Briny is third chair soprano sax. Cardiff Castle by Mark Williams. America the Beautiful. Rock Around the Clock. *Going home, going home, Lord I'm going home.* And the German band part of the Ninth Symphony.

We're close. I can see Briny's fingers only, just above in my line of vision the first chair guy's, Stuart Howell, who was born to play sax, slouched into perfection by the god of the blues. His and Briny's fingers do exactly the same. And this is the very day by the way bye the bye that Briny's four year-old brother Tuck has learned how to whistle. He has been at it since he woke up, and all through the concert he does his soft and breathy pursed accompaniment, lips pointed straight at his older sister's horn section, except when he turns to us to smile, which is often.

You cannot smile and whistle at the same time. It is impossible, and ineffable that during the screaks and huffing of Schiller's Ode to Joy the Berlin Philharmonic and Herbert von Karajan in his cloak of majestic art come rising through the caramel off-brown metal folding chairs, and I hear Tuck piping a spontaneous anthem for the anti-war movement. There is, and you can rely on it, genius in such auditory splatterpaint exhaustion.

We eventually release from the mangle of music and wire and paper cups to sit awhile quietly in the parking lot inside our cars with the windows rolled up, somewhat peaceful, but fuddled with how the too-many things going on at once got this bad. As a world or nation, as a county or a self, we must begin to take one day of silence a week, a month, to steamhose the brain-hallways clean of pixilgrime.

The Sound Made by Snapping
the Fingers

finger releasing finger
would not seem to make
such sound, but it do

the middle one pretends to contend
with the thumb, then slides off
to hit the meaty part of the heel
of the palm, but none of those
mechanics is where the sound
comes from

the clear note arrives
from the invisible, some
inches apart from the act,
coming in on airy cellphone
lines from Polynesia, South Africa,
and Central Asia, where body
percussion is musically
honored as language

my Sri Lankan teacher, Bawa
Muhaiyaddeen, sitting on his bed,
as he always was when I knew him, once
looked at me sitting on the bedroom
floor, said, Some people grow beards
and stand in front of crowds
pretending to be wise

said, some people make their living
so easily, just by snapping
their fingers, like this,
like that, like this

they are wrong, those who say
it is harder to work with your brain
than with your hands   they are wrong

no matter   the loveliest way of going
is to do almost nothing, make only
a slight sound, be as empty as
a piece of paper with nothing on it
take a nightwalk   and then rest

Losing It

Before conscious memory, before language
gave me these unsatisfactory terms
for saying who I am and how emotions
are flowing through, everything
I had to lose was whole.

Now I am seventy, full of doubt-fragments
of rage and tenderness,
and I have had a vision of frightening
forgetfulness, a dream
on August 11th.

This is how it goes. I am in an urban conference
setting, walking in and out
of wide hallways and those huge meeting rooms
with adjustible walls.

I am confused and have no short-term memories
to locate myself with. It is a very convincing sense
of how it may feel to have had a stroke.

Then I am in a car, driving,
with a man in the passenger seat talking.

I have no recall as to who he is, how we got here,
or what he is talking about. I am driving,
going nowhere that I know.

Now in the dream I am seated at a table
of restored consciousness
with this awareness we have here,
the connection to time and space,
with this sharing through the eyes
a knowledge of who we are, and where,
and a few ingenious guesses as to why.

Such beautiful companionship
holds that table of bright being.

A man at the other end, a friend in the spirit,
no one known actually, he looks at me
seeing the grief and terror I have just felt

for my diminished consciousness.
He reaches his hand toward me acknowledging the grief.
I hold his fingers. That was the dream.

Now at another table, not in any dream,
a round restaurant table. I come along an aisle.
They see me first
and put paper napkins up to hide their faces
except for the eyes, like muslim women,
like harem princesses, like train robbers.

It is my son Benjamin, 42, and his two children,
Briny, 14, and Tuck, 7.
I sit down and tell them the dream.
Then announce that I shall recite
an Emily Dickinson poem that I have just last night
memorized, proof I have not lost it yet.

> God made a little gentian.

I explain what they may not know
that a gentian is a blue flower that blooms
in late November. Some of them grow
in a little dell near my cabin.

At the appointed time each year I go out,
as a poet must, and there they are,
deep imperial blue, the size
of Christmas bulbs glowing.

> God made a little gentian.
> It tried to be a rose and failed.
> And all the summer laughed.
> But just before the snows
>
> There rose a purple creature
> That ravished all the hill,
> And summer hid her forehead
> And mockery was still.

Pause, longpause.

> The frosts were her condition.

That's the best line.

So far, yes it is, says Briny.

Now I lose the thread completely
of the poem's going.

      The frosts were her condition.

Pause. I am very close to cursing
in front of my grandchildren.

      God made a little gentian, I repeat.

      God made a little snowman, says Benjamin.
      Frosty was his name, says Tuck.

      His nose was drippy and his eyes
      were cruel and insane, says Briny.

They're going round the table.

      He romped and played the tuba.
      No one could keep him quiet.

      They sent him to Aruba
      And put him on a rice diet.

Grow still thy mockery,
I chime in grand poetic tone.

So I shall now paraphrase
what I cannot precisely
at this moment quote.

      The lady would not put on her purple dress,
      until this relative from up North called,
      somewhere near Chicago, to suggest
      she should get out more, join a bookclub
      or learn French. No need to be chained
      to an apartment like a park bench to a pole.

Now the Tyrian, ah the Tyrian from Tyre,
it comes back, ancient coastal town
down where now is brutal Lebanon.

Tyre and Sidon, twin sources
for the beach mollusc dye
so prized by royalty, indigo
with streaks of crimson.

The Tyrian would not come,
and why should she, really.

The Tyrian would not come
until the North invoke it.

Wait for it, wait,
Emily's poignant final question,
so late arising in November.

Creator, shall I bloom?

Thus to openly satirize granddaddy
loudly and unanimously,
when he shall more obviously
be losing it than now

may be a way to finish dinner
without having to sit in silence
while he weeps for his forgetting

God's goddam little gentian
that nobody can remember how
or where he used to put it.

This is not the end.
We shall use the gentian
for a blue flower torch
through the dark of this
into whatever is next.

The sky's deep blue before it goes black,
darkest dew-soaked shade, my friend,
this love at the last
that does not want to leave.

Even with time no longer in the mix,
we grow more awake in the night of it,
this lovelike lake filling with snowmelt.

520

God made a little Gentian –
It tried – to be a Rose –
And failed – and all the Summer laughed –
But just before the Snows

There rose a Purple Creature –
That ravished all the Hill –
And Summer hid her Forehead –
And Mockery – was still –

The Frosts were her condition –
The Tyrian would not come
Until the North – invoke it –
Creator – Shall I – bloom?

JUST THIS ONCE

Just This Once

President Bush, before you order airstrikes,
imagine the first cruise
missile as a direct hit on your closest friend.

That might be Laura. Then twenty-five other
family and friends.
There are no survivors. Now imagine some

other way to do it. Quadruple the inspectors.
Put a thousand and one
U.N. people in. Then call for peace activists

to volunteer to go to Iraq for two weeks each.
Flood that country with
well-meaning tourists, people curious about

the land that produced the great saints, Gilani,
Hallaj, and Rabia.
Set up hostels near those tombs. Encourage peace

people to spend a bunch of money in shops, to bring
rugs home and samovars
by the bushel. Send an Arabic translator with

every four activists. The U.S. government will pay
for the translators and for
building and staffing the hostels, one hostel for

every twenty visitors and five translators. Central
air and heat are state of the art,
and the hostels belong to the Iraqis at the end

of this experiment. Pilgrims with carpentry skills
will add studios, porches,
ramadas, meditation cribs on the roof, clerestories,

and lots of subtle color. Jimmy Carter, Nelson
Mandela, and my friend,
Jonathan Granoff at the U.N., will be the core

organizational team. Abdul Aziz Said too has got
to be in on this, who
grew up in a Bedouin tent four hundred miles

east of Damascus. He didn't see a table until
he was fourteen. Shamans
from various traditions, Martin Prechtal,

Bly, and many powerful women, Sima Simar,
Debra, Naomi, Jane.
I offer these exalted services without having

asked anybody. No one knows what might come
of such potlatch, potluck.
Maybe nothing, or maybe it would show some

of the world that we really do not wish to kill
anybody and that we
truly are not out to appropriate oil reserves.

We're working on building a hydrogen vehicle
as fast as we can, aren't we?
Put no limit on the number of activists from all

over that might want to hang out and explore Iraq
for two weeks. Is anything
left of Babylon? There could be informal courses

for college credit and pickup soccer games every
evening at five. Long
leisurely late suppers. Chefs will come for cookouts.

The U.S. government furnishes air transportation,
that is, hires airliners from
the country of origin and back for each peace tourist,

who must carry and spend the equivalent of $1001
US inside Iraq. Keep part
of the invasion force nearby as police, but let those

who claim to deeply detest war try something else
just this once, for one year.
Call our bluff. Medical services, transportation

inside Iraq, along with many other ideas that
will be thought of later
during the course of this innocently, blatantly

foolish project will all also be funded by
the U.S. government. But what
if terrible unforeseen disaster rains down

because of this spontaneous, unthought-out
hippie notion? One
never knows. Surely it wouldn't be worse

than the *shock and awe* display we have planned
for the first forty-eight hours.
But we must always suspect intentionally good

deeds. Consider this more of a lark, a skylark.
Look. There is
a practice known as *sema*, the deep listening

to poetry and music, with sometimes movement
involved. Unpremeditated
art and ease. We could experiment with whole

nights of that, staying up till dawn, sleeping
in tents during the day.
Good musicians will be lured with more than

modest fees. Cellos, banjos, oboes, ouds,
French horns. Hundreds
of harmonicae and the entire University

of North Carolina undergraduate gospel choir.
Thus instead of war
there is much relaxed, improvisational festivity

from March 2003 through February 2004. It could be
as though war had already
happened, as it has. And now we're in the giddy,

brokenopen aftertime. So let slip the pastel
minivans of peace and whoa
be they who cry surcease. I'll be first to

volunteer for two weeks of wandering winter desert
reading Hallaj, Abdul Qadir
Gilani, dear Rabia, and Scherazade's life-prolonging

thousand and one *Arabian Nights*. I am Coleman Barks,
retired English professor eeee-
meritus, living in Athens, Georgia, and I don't

really consider this proposal foolish. More brash
and hopeful for the bunch
I come along with, those born from the mid-1920's

until the mid-1940's, that before we die or lose
our energy, we might,
with help from tablas, sitar, waterwheeling

sixteen-strings, and the pulsing voice of seventy
black-church-bred students push away
from terrorism and cruise missile terrorism

and the video-techno-laser, loveless, unerotic-
idiotic, bio-chemo atom-toys,
and decide not to study war so much no more.

Never denying we have the tendencies built-in,
a cold murderous
aggression, a who-cares-it's-all-bullshit-

anyway turning away from those in pain. March
15th, 2003, and I am not
quite yet weary enough of words not to try

to say the taste of this failure we sponsor
with our tax dollars,
but after the stupidity starts, I might be.

The Harrier Commander's Video

I am watching televsion in a hotel room
in Bristol, England, during the Kosovo bombardment.

The foreground buildings are not
the primary target. They remain intact,
you see. Now. Quite a secondary explosion,
munitions undoubtedly. Good work there.

In this case, a US tomahawk missile has gone off course.
True. This was Pavo Remi's remote farmhouse.
The left side of the roof and Pavo's head
are removed instantly before the missile
fully impacts in the sheep pen, reducing it,
as you see, to a hole fifty feet deep.
One of the children, a three-year-old girl,
is unharmed. The others are in various stages
of dying. The wife, the mother, slashed open
by a split house-joist and a piece
of the hot water heater. Closeups of carnage,
unrecognizable bandage piles that are what's
left of the other four children.

I just want you to see what happens.
He cannot stop himself. Tax dollars at work.
He pushes the pointer handle
into his stomach and moans.

This kind of coverage never happens
in the United States, cannot happen,
because the thirty-five people in charge
of what gets shown on television news
self-censor themselves. This is my theory.
It may be more governmentally sent down
through channels than that.

Here some years later, a video
has been circling the internet
since April 2004 when the events happened.
Aaron Brown put some of it briefly
on a segment October 12th.

A street is seen from the air,
a conversation between two American young men,
jet pilot and forward observer. We do not know
where the observer is in relation to the street.
Forty people moving along in Fallujah,
not running, walking quickly,
though we cannot see any detail. They are
blurs. They look like women in burqahs.
The pilot asks should he take them out.
The observer says quickly, *Take them out.*
Silence. Then, *Ten seconds.* A dustcloud
covers everything. A five hundred pound
bomb has obliterated the figures.
Dude, says the pilot's voice.

American College Students Overheard in a Restaurant After I Return from Afghanistan

I would love to make out with you.

My best friend.

All he does is get drunk.

I would love to get him drunk. I will buy him drinks all night long.

I am so sweet you would not believe.

I just want to sleep with him, but he won't let me touch him.

Darlin. Ashby. You have to do it subtly.

If I was his girl, I'd be home with him right now. It would be like bye, y'all.

It's getting stormy outside.

Shut up.

I wear clothes that fit my body type.

I don't like this outfit. I want to go change.

Nooooo. No.   No.

If you say can I buy you a shot, he'll take it. You have to be direct. I have money. Keep buying.

Where is everybody?

Everybody's gone next door trying to get laid.

Stormy's like covered.

If you're looking for a brother, that he's not.

I would be all, I mean, all over her. Really.

I love my girlfriend.

Y'all going to get married?

Potato pancakes.

You can wait with me.

Not that Tommy, the one that works at Dino's.

What do you think?

I am so invisible. They cannot possibly. Here they come.

I love you.

I love you too.

Will you marry me?

If you have a ring.

I can get one.

You work on that.

Stern Mystics and Secret Governmental Murder, An Introduction to Osho Rajneesh's Sanai book, Unio Mystica I

A TOAST FOR HAKIM SANAI

Sanai's tone is distinct from Rumi's, tougher. There is a challenging feel to the poetry. He awakens more by accusation than by gentle guidance. The soul-quality of his teacher, Lai-Kur, comes through, and all we know of Lai-Kur is a toast he once proposed, two toasts actually.

Hakim Sanai was attached to the court of the King of Ghazna in the Persian empire of the mid-12th Century. The king was setting out on a pointless military expedition to India. Sanai was along to write the conventional laudatory record. That is what a court poet did. He wrote poems in praise of his patron, never critical. PR for the reigning regime.The expedition was riding by a walled garden, from behind which came beautiful music and singing. They looked over the wall. It was Lai-Kur, drinking wine and singing. He stood and proposed a toast, To the blindness of the King!

What do you mean?

Bahramshah is going on this ridiculous expedition to India when he is needed here at home, and besides, what he is looking for is in himself.

Lai-Kur then proposed another toast. To the even greater blindness of Hakim Sanai!

Please explain, said Sanai looking into the luminous eyes of the Sufi master.

You are unaware of the purpose of your life. You will come into God's presence with these silly poems, commending various political stupidities.

Sanai immediately felt the truth of Lai-Kur. He left the service of Bahramshah and went on pilgrimage. The king desperately tried to lure him back, offering even his daughter's hand and half the wealth of the kingdom. But Sanai was unshakeable in his new state. This refusal profoundly disturbed the king, because, obviously, he had been given the same darshan from Lai-Kur but had been unable to make any change in his life. The meaningless, wasteful invasion of India continued as planned.

Sanai came back from his pilgrimage with the text of the *Hadiqa, The Walled Garden of Truth*. We feel in it the lightning that struck and galvanized the court poet into the soul-work of his being.

These two volumes of morning talks given by Osho Rajneesh to his community in Pune, India, contain brilliant commentary on various passages from Sanai's *Hadiqa,* using David Pendlebury's 1974 English translation. Osho approaches the Sufi master from the inside out; that is, he speaks of Sanai's beauty and wisdom from within his own enlightenment. This is not literary explication. It is more like friend speaking of friend. Osho uses Sanai's text as a kind of grace, an attunement through which he converys his own intelligent openness of being. A great range of subjects comes up, from the crux of this moment in history, twenty-five centuries after the Buddha's enlightenment, to whether it is more difficult for a man or a woman to decide to take *sannyas* (the ultimate commitment to a teacher.)

I did not take sannyas with Osho. When I visited the commune in Pune in October of 1988, I already had a deep connection with a teacher, Bawa Muhaiyaddeen. I have told that story in other places (see p. 140 of *Rumi: The Book of Love*). One moment, though, that I have not included yet in any account—I just recently remembered it—is this: Bawa said to me that sometimes one has a mirror to see the front and a mirror behind to see the back. Two reflections are needed to see both sides, implying that I would have two teachers. Bawa told me to do the Rumi work in 1978 (It must be done.) Osho said in 1988, This is beautiful poetry. It has to be because it is coming from Rumi's love, but you must watch out for it, Professor Coleman. For you, it can become ecstatic self-hypnosis. He nailed me with that hit, and I am grateful for the guidance of both masters. I am still trying to assimilate the wisdom. I may be the only person to have had both Bawa Muhaiyaddeen and Osho as teachers. They are so different. But in one matter they are similar. Neither wanted followers. That is not what I was or am. I just need, and accept, all the help I can get.

THE BIG PICTURE

John Keats is right. This is a vale of soulmaking. Some planetary collective awareness is continually building, along with the tribal, personal, familial, national, and neighborhood consciousnesses. They trickle, pour, drip-drop, and thunder down through each other, altering the consistency and intensity of who we are and what we know and feel. *Soul* is the usual hapless word we throw at this process.

In the 1950s I took college courses in intellectual history. They were very fine, taught by the eccentric James Hall in the History Department at Chapel Hill. But they feel inadequate to the truth of the matter now. All the talk of -isms, Marxism, romanticism, Darwinism, and no talk at all of the mystics and the artists. The geniuses of William Blake, Emily Dickinson, Whitman, Melville, Oscar Wilde, Hopkins, and Neitzsche surely shaped the 19th Century as it came forward and became the 20th, and now the 21st. Only Wilde and Whitman and Neitzsche of those were recognized in their times as having creative value. I contend that Osho will come to be seen as such a germane, yeasty presence in our soul fermentation. Freud, Jung, Einstein, Joseph Campbell, Cormac McCarthy, Groucho Marx, the quiet tenderness of James Wright, the brilliant cultural surgery of Robert Bly, many elements will come forward as we look back. Osho will be one of them. The history of soulmakers is our most significant history. They are the moving indices of how we say our truth. That is why it is so important to examine the circumstances leading to Osho's death in 1990.

CONFESSIONS OF A DANGEROUS MIND

These are times that try men's souls, says Thomas Paine in one of his firebrand pamphlets that shaped our democracy, such as it is. The times are still wearing us down. It feels more like we have government *of* multinational corporations, *by* vested interests, *for* the many secret agencies. The People are out in the street, but not much in the picture. The media barely covers war protests. I saw a movie recently that gives me some hope, "Confessions of a Dangerous Mind." It is Chuck Barris' story, and I take it as a thinly disguised documentary, a true account of how the CIA hired him to kill thirty-three people during the Cold War.

What emerges in the film is a new American type that may not yet have a name. Part Melville's confidence man, part Cormac McCarthy's judge in *Blood Meridian*. Serial killer and innocent abroad. Carnival barker secret agent. Barris was the goofball genius who thought of The Gong Show, The Dating Game, The Newlyweds, and god knows what else, P. T. Barnum and 007. New Age guru and ungovernable operative. Barris appears as himself at the end of this movie he directed, still alive and looking wise enough to face this ugly truth.

There have been other movies about the spook hitmen of the CIA but this one has the raw provocation of Thomas Paine. Our tax dollars paid a gameshow host to kill thirty-three people for various anti-communist reasons (I guess). How many others are there like Chuck Barris? Twenty? Two thousand? Can *The History of American Secret Agencies, Vols. 1-12*, ever be written? It is naive to even ask for that. Who determines who will be killed next and why? We may never know. This movie opens the issue.

I say a democracy must not run *permanently* secret operations, or it will become something other than a democracy. Effective checks and balances must exist. Of course, there must be a way to have secure missions in wartime, during criminal investigations, stings, terrorist surveillance, etc. There are certainly valid reasons for a government not to say all that it is doing, but at some point there has to be some way of knowing what we have done, who did what, how the chain of command went. Either we have an elected chief calling these shots, or some unelected appointed underling is authorizing murder by personal whim.

The Murder of Osho by the U.S. Government

If the U.S. government used tax money to assassinate an enlightened being, I would like to trace the methodology. I have no doubt that there are secret whackings for trivial, policy, reasons. But this is different. Osho Rajneesh was assassinated for his worldview. Fundamentalist orthodoxies have ever opposed, and even killed, innovators who break with the past. Hallaj, Jesus, Suhrawardi. If this is our orthodoxy I want to hold it up to the light. Tom Robbins assessed the perceived threat of Osho by the Reagan administration like this. "Government authorities intuitively sense something dangerous in his message, something that can set men and women loose from their control. Nothing frightens the state, or its partner in crime, organized religion, so much as the prospect of a population thinking for itself and living free."

When I began this introduction, I had intended to reveal with specifics how Tom Robbins' theory played out in this instance. I don't know who I thought I was. The research needed would take years, require a covert team of counter-espionage experts, moles, a huge budget, silencers, exile, and cunning. None of which I have energy or resources for.

There are several books that will be helpful to anyone wishing to pursue this matter, and someone should. *Was Rajneesh (Osho) Poisoned by Ronald Reagan's America?* by Sue Appleton and Max Brecher's *A Passage to America.* I have looked into those two. A lot of careful investigation went into them. There are specific names and places, uncovered while the trail was still hot and memories fresh, that could be followed up on. I sense that Max Brecher is being as factual as he possibly can be, and to go on record, for what it is worth, it looks like to me that Osho was poisoned by some faction of the powers-that-be. I have met his doctor, George Meredith (Amrito), and I believe him. Amrito supervised the thallium tests. He says that Osho's health changed radically after that strange interlude, about a week, he spent alone in an Oklahoma jail in November of 1985, while supposedly being taken from Charlotte to Seattle for deportation back to India. Thallium is an untraceable (after a year) heavy metal, but the symptoms of thallium poisoning are clearly set forth in the medical literature. Osho developed most if not all of them, and he had exhibited none of them prior to November 1985. I am no scholar of the evidence, but I do believe he was murdered by the U.S government. Someone else will have to present the full case. We need for whoever put the thallium in Osho's jail food to come forward and tell who ordered him to do that. Nobody need be punished. Nothing can help the situation now, but it would be healthy for us to know the truth. Most probably the villain was Reagan, dead now, and the victim, Osho, is fine ash and spirit.

I am grateful for the chance to say this outrage publically, even if embedded in an introduction to spontaneous talks on passages from an obscure Sufi poet. Hakim Sanai would certainly approve. Another toast then, pure springwater this time, to some of the true mystics, Sanai, Osho, Bawa, Lai-Kur, Rumi, and Shams Tabriz, our garden on the ruins.

The Time Needed

Years are needed before the sun
working on a Yemeni rock
can make a bloodstone ruby.

Months must pass before cotton seed
can provide a seamless shroud.

Days go by before a handful of wool
becomes a halter rope.

Decades it takes a child
to change into a poet.

And civilizations fall and are ploughed under
to grow a garden on the ruins,
a true mystic.

—HAKIM SANAI

Soulmaking and the Coming Bomb

Two observations. We are not separate. Consciousness plays and builds inside each, and in the collective. That insight gets explored in Jung and Joseph Campbell's work, and in Rumi's evolutionary consciousness passages: I was a mineral; then I died and became a plant; then I died and became an animal, then human, then an enlightened human, on to the unimaginable next phase. What have I ever lost by dying?

Secondly, conversational telepathy is present. Driving north out of L.A., she tells me her last night's dream of already launched missiles. Meditators are meditating precisely where the bombs will land. They know this, and there is time for them to save themselves, but they will not leave. In the dream she thinks they are foolish. She relinquishes them to their choiceless passivity, leaving the scene, knowing in a few moments they will all be dead.

I am listening to her as we drive the freeway and wondering about the building complex on the far ridge, remembering the open letter the Dalai Lama sent to President Bush on September 12th, 2001, asking him to consider a nonviolent response. A scene comes to my mind of Patti Smith stomping her foot and yelling, *1959! 1959!* The year Chinese communists took over Tibet, the terrible massacres there, and the Dalai Lama's exile to Dharmsala, India.

I remain quiet until she says, Patti Smith played last week at the Getty, which answers my *unspoken* question about the buildings and enters my reverie about the necessity for action versus the pull toward nonviolence and contemplation. In the driving along we have been talking *telepathically*. This is going on all the time, and most likely all over the place. Which is not to deny that the aloneness we feel is absolute. It is.

I met Lee Butler once in a hotel lobby. I put my hand on my heart and bowed, You are the hope of the world, Lee Butler. For a number of years he was the commander of SAC, our Stretegic Air Command. They would run test situations that he could not know whether they were real or not. Thirty-seven times he heard himself say, *Full retaliatory response, Mr. President.* Then he quit. He goes around now lecturing, urging immediate and total nuclear disarmament. No human being must *ever* be given the power to say those five words, which could destroy much, if not all, of the intricate flowering of awareness on this blue planet. Lee Butler is clear about that.

Thich Nhat Hanh gave a talk about anger at the Riverside Church in New York on September 25, 2001, remembering Ben Tre, his hometown, an ancient South Vietnamese city of 300,000, which incidentally, is exactly the size of Chattanooga, where I grew up in the 1940's. North Vietnamese guerrillas coming through had launched shoulder-fired aircraft missiles at U.S. planes. They hit nothing, then faded into the surrounding landscape. A Special Forces colonel ordered massive carpet bombing completely demolishing Ben Tre. He is famous for saying, *I had to destroy the city to save it.* He was serious. And insane for the moment in the way people often become in war. Remember Chattanooga.

Thich Nhat Hanh felt angry about the order that turned his hometown to powder. In New York that morning he was angry about the World Trade Center. The number of 9/11 dead, of course, was much less than the tens of thousands dead in Ben Tre. Thich Nhat Hanh had a meditation practice. Watching the mind, he says, helps to bring him through such events without his anger causing more suffering. It is difficult to get reliable estimates on what we have done numerically, how many we killed, say, in the first Gulf War. Four hundred thousand is one figure. Three hundred and ninety-seven thousand more than 9/11. Such numbers are rarely mentioned in the news. They are numbers, I think, crucial to planetary sanity.

I was born in 1937, too young for Korea, too old for Vietnam. I have not experienced war. Only in the movies. Still, with no credentials, I advise us to keep talking and talking until we're blue in the face to try and avoid going to war. My son Benjamin at thirty-eight, in his tremendously powerful body, got hit recently, struck with fists and elbows, pushed down, and kicked by a group of white skinhead punks. He had been talking cars with them late at night standing out on a side street under a streetlight in Athens, Georgia. He is a total motorhead expert. There was no argument. They just started hitting him. He did not hit back. He kept asking, *Why are you doing this? Why!* They had no answer. It was just the time of night when after they had been drinking beer, they beat up on somebody. I am so proud of him for not reacting to the absurd attack. He could have sent several to the hospital. His response was difficult and brilliant. It is crazy out there on the street, as well as here inside, in the human psyche. Talking did not work that time.

September 1988, Taos, New Mexico. I am at the dusty bus station with a friend, leaving for Nepal and India after three weeks at the Wurlitzer Art Colony. I am fifty-one. Kathy, my friend, is twenty-six, a tri-athlete with broad muscular shoulders and short-cropped swimmer's hair. She could easily be mistaken for a man. She and I are not lovers, just good buddies. She grew up with four older brothers. Her way of being affectionate is to punch me on the shoulder, hard, and get punched. We are like a couple of teenage boys shouldering against each other in the parking lot. Hugging too, in the goodbye tenderness of sundown. She is staying longer in Taos. She has given me a ride to the bus station.

A wiry, slightly drunk, hispanic man walks over. I've got something to say to you people. Strange cold eyes. What's that? yells Kathy from the midst of her wrestling bumptiousness. Do you know what you are? No, what are we? Yelling at close range now. I sense then how he is seeing us, as some new version of homosexuality that must be confronted in this public forum. He sees me seeing that, realizes that I am not gay, and begins in his new confusion spouting venomous Spanish. I turn Kathy away and walk her into the bus lobby. The guy is shooing us with his arms as though he has harried us from a field of combat, matador bastard. Do you know that guy? I ask a man behind the desk. He doesn't. Shithead gets back in the passenger side of an old blue pickup. I stand in the bus station door with suddenly enraged adrenalin surging through me. This is how a manslaughter charge begins. I point directly at him, long and hard and definite, *you sonofabitch*. He leans to get out; a blue work-shirted arm comes across holding him inside the truck.

Who knows what might have happened. Neither of us could have backed down at that point in our chemistry lesson. War needs to be stopped by an outside party. I have never been in a real fight without boxing gloves. All I would know how to do is run at him like I did as a blocking back in football, try to run him over with knees and elbows. It might have worked, but he might have had a knife, or a gun, or a martial arts skill. I am grateful we did not have to live through the stupidity we called down on ourselves. The sunset glare on half the windshield kept me from seeing who saved me and my

Spanish-speaking adversary from our bullring pretentions. We have been allowed to go fumblingly along these last twenty years with most of our faculties intact, and hopefully with more sympathy, more tenderness than we had that late afternoon in 1988. It is for lack of those emotions, and with a great incapacity for grief, that we go to war. I would like to meet the man now and see how he remembers the incident. We could sit in a bar and laugh about it. We could meditate together. Yawn. If as a civilization we are going to be saved from the plausible scenarios so easy to imagine, surely some of us *alive now* must find a way to become intuitive and unenraged enough, ungreedy enough, to be part of the saving, like that merciful, wise, blue, longsleeved cottonshirted arm was for me and my friend.

Charlotte Rotterdam, former head of curriculum at Naropa, tells me a dream she had some months before September 11th. She is in a plane flying through the skyscraper canyons of New York. The plane slides into a building; people caught in an elevator are frantically trying to talk to her, reaching out. She cannot hear what they are saying, but she is aware that she should not approach them, because they are dead. She cannot help. Some compassion in her, outside-of-time, came to the scene early and observed the horror. We do have visionary skills. Maybe they will help us not to self-destruct.

Sam Seawright, a New York artist, tells about his friend, Michael Richards, whose story has appeared, with pictures, in the *NY Times* and the *Village Voice*. Sam shared a studio for five years with Michael. That September Michael was doing a residency in the World Trade Center with a studio on the 92nd floor. He worked an all-nighter September 10th. One of the sculptures in his studio was a lifesize, silvery bronze cast of himself, slim, tall, powerful, proportioned very like the towers themselves. All one burnished glow, hands by his side, palms opening out; his wideopen eyes staring into another dimension. He is in a flight suit floating a foot off the ground. The fusilages of nine planes are disappearing into his torso, in the chest-heart area. People gasp when they see pictures of it now. Michael conceived the sculpture as a tribute to the heroic black pilots in WWI, the Tuskegee Airmen. Michael was a young artist from Harlem in his late thirties just on the edge of moving into his power and wider recognition. We have pictures of the sculpture, but no trace of the artwork or the artist, both destroyed in 9/11. In the mystery of his soulmaking Michael

Richards knew what was coming.

But maybe another bomb is not coming. Remember all the crawling under school desks we did, and the creepy, stocked suburban bomb shelters? Six-thirty p.m., August 6th, 1945, I am coming out of the dining hall at Baylor School, where my father is headmaster. I am eight. A staggered pile of evening papers, the *Chattanooga News Free Press,* are on the entryway floor with big block-letters, ATOM BOMB ATOM BOMB. I stare down at the words, not knowing what an atom bomb is. Nor do I now. Who would have bet that no other nuclear device would be exploded in a conflict for the next sixty-three years? Who will bet we will go another sixty-three?

Should we live as though non-use will continue indefinitely? Who would seriously propose that? Yet that is how we are effectively acting. Attempts at nuclear disarmament are proceeding. I support them. But at seventy, ten years retired from teaching, I rarely go to meetings and mostly save my money for the grandchildren. Every so often I send the Peace Tax Fund a check. That is a bill in Congress that would allow taxpayers to check a box on their income tax forms if they do not want *their* monies to go for armament, but rather go for education, health care, poverty. It is a very quiet and VERY radical idea. I carry and give away ballpoint pens from *majority.org* that have a pull-out feature showing how disproportionate Pentagon spending is compared to what goes for more humane purposes, the huge discrepancy, *five times as much.* Double that with Iraq. That's about the extent of my activism.

Meditation, inner work, is crucial, but I decline to join the sitting ducks of the earlier dream. I am not a pacifist yet, but I am getting closer. Violence does always beget more violence, and in war, *everybody* becomes one of *the bad guys* we hear so much about. That last is a new and powerful idea from Howard Zinn's *Just War.* It has been suggested we not watch any more screen-images of men running somewhere with guns drawn to solve some situation, that we turn off the elation of our overwhelming, shock-and-awe firepower. There go the westerns and the war movies. Let's try to move the violent mechanisms to one side, and keep on talking, as Faulkner hoped we would, through everything, until the last ding-dong of doom. Jimmy Carter is the tireless hero of this obvious, but most difficult-to-sustain, strategy of conflict resolution.

I went to ground zero. It was so cold and windy we could not stay long on the observation platform, February 4th, 2002, my friend Ed Hicks and myself and just a very few others. Workers were loading *frozen earth* into dump trucks. I am told they rarely find even a faucet or a doorknob, everything being ground so fine. Ed and I walk the twenty-two blocks back to the Chelsea Hotel. That was good talking. What can we do other than talk? Jonathan Granoff has solid suggestions. First and most quickly, we must inventory and protect, and eventually destroy, all nuclear bombmaking materials on the entire planet. We must search out and destroy as well the other weapons of mass destruction, the materials, the labs, necessary to produce the terror we sense is coming, as well as our *terrible* responses to it. Nuclear, chemical, biological, cyber, and combinations not yet thought of. This may be impossibly naive, utopian, but so was abolitionist talk in the 1830s. We *must begin* to talk in new, strange, impossible ways, before being forced to by the radical cruelties of a next event. *Not* to begin would be more cynical than we can tolerate. Keeping such weapons out of anybody's hands is common sense and must become the overriding agenda of the United Nations. One Sunday night in the fall I was walking to my coffeehouse. A group of middleaged people were sitting out on an open porch in a circle, lots of rocking chairs. Candles placed around. They were talking quietly. I could not hear. Gatherings are happening we do not know about. It is possible we can learn to share our bewilderment and come to some confusing agreement.

Muslim suicide bombers are about as full of soul as a passed-out American wino is full of spirit. Their explosions are equally as obscene as our child-deafening daisy-cutters and skinhead sneering. I have looked in the compassionate eyes of a *qutb*. I do not want to act from coldness. I want to look through *those* eyes, Bawa Muhaiyaddeen's. We inhabit something like an ocean or a presence, though there are no likenesses, or names, for the all-connecting mystery, and I bring no proof of it other than everybody's individual awareness, and the universe. How could one prove that such a habitat as this is sacred and beautiful? It is too close. We live within the jasmine evidence.

Twenty per cent of the world is Islamic, one in five. What percentage sees the West as a dangerous contaminant to their culture? What percentage rejoiced in the moment of 9/11 and still considers those involved as martyrs? Is it 5%? 25%? One one-thousandth of 1%? The last percentage would amount to twenty-five hundred people. The 25% would be five hundred million. Somewhere in between? More? A Gallup poll says 61% (or it may be 75%) of *all* muslims believe that no Arabs were involved in 9/11, that it was done either by the U.S. or Israel or both.

I have walked a little in the Islamic world and felt its deep compassion and courtesy. Farmers going to noon prayers in the town of Hajji Bektas in central Turkey. I loved walking with those men, and sitting with the Sufi circles in Istanbul and Konya. I have fancied myself a bridge between cultures (every human being is such a bridge), the Islamic mystics and the no-church, no-doctrine ecstatics of the American Sublime, which is indigenous and worldwide. We sing one song about how this is a sacred place, a mystery worth praising and studying with minute loving attention. Something in us knows what the Sufis so extravagantly chant, that *everything* is God. No matter what destruction comes, no matter what delight, it is all THAT. I had a dream on the night before 9/11. My friend, the Irish playwright Tom MacIntyre, and I were looking for the airport. We could not find it. We had a plane to catch. We went into a kitchen. There were pots of violets everywhere, beautiful violets. We went through the kitchen and out the back door still looking for the elusive airport. End of dream. I take it as a pre-sensing of the airport violence/violets that was cooking in the collective kitchen. I was leaving Toronto that Tuesday morning and did have great difficulty finding the airport. When I finally got to the car rental return, I walked into where everyone was stunned-silent watching the television high on the wall. The second tower was falling live with Michael Richards in it.

Thinking of ways to keep ourselves from fighting is not nearly so exciting as war and the crank-up roar of those machines. The imagining of war, not the experience. My grandsons, Tuck and Woody, by all appearances, are warlords-in-training. They have all the fantasy equipment, the stance and the moves. I was in the presence of a warlord once, March 2005. Mohammad Atta (!), Governor of Bactria, the northern sector of Afghanistan. He wanted to know how I had liked the *bouskashi* I had seen earlier that day. Three-four hundred ferocious men on stallions in a full-gallop colliding over a dead calf filled with sand. Damnedest upper-body strength sport I ever saw. I waxed on about the manly recklessness, as he smiled his camaraderie. Testosterone forever, bro. So let us have nuclear disarmament, and plenty of *boushkashi*.

A Palestinian girl straps on her tenpenny bomb belt, walks in among Israeli kids just like her and changes her mind. She goes through the whole suicide bomber drill, makes a martyrdom video, then decides not to. Through a sequence of events I do not know, the girl is currently in an Israeli jail. They should have given her a cabinet position, say Minister of Tourism, or at a lower level, Director of the experimental Arab-Israeli comedy troupe which will do improvised street theatre this fall. Lots of vests that release balloons and roses, effigy skits, bloated generals, holocaust humor. Enter a VW bug with painted windows.

Meeting of Poet and President

There is a passage in *Specimen Days*, August 12, 1863; here it is
August 12, 2001, a hundred and thirty-eight years later, not so long.
From his upstairs room near Vermont and L in Washington the poet
tells of seeing the president every morning riding in to the White
House from where he spends the night, for the coolness, at a
soldiers' home three miles north of the city.

"I saw him this morning about eight-thirty. He always has a
company of twenty-five or so cavalry, with sabres drawn and held
upright over their shoulders. Mr. Lincoln generally rides a good-
sized, easy-going grey horse, is dressed in plain black, somewhat
rusty and dusty, wears a stiff black hat and looks about as ordinary
in attire as the commonest man. I see very plainly Abraham
Lincoln's dark brown face with the deep-cut lines, the eyes, always
to me with a latent sadness. We have got so that we exchange bows,
and very cordial ones."

Sometimes one of his sons, a boy of ten or twelve, accompanies him,
riding at his right on a pony. "They passed me once very close, and I
saw the president in the face fully; his look, though abstracted,
happen'd to be directed steadily in my eye. He bowed and smiled,
but far beneath his smile I noticed well the expression I have
alluded to."

Lincoln's grief-eyes meeting Whitman's joy and wondering has a
great range of palette in the mix. The paint smears to muddy rose
with yellow streaks and polkadots of grey-green, cobalt. Whitman's
exuberant, always erotic, watching, the wisdom of his excess:
Lincoln's kind, saturnine, slightly tickled, grin. Those days before
cars, electricity, August air-conditioning, and, seemingly with the
polished sabres, before guns, but not. There was the horrible, point-
blank, head-removing cannonfire going on, and these two bowing
faces, stupified with the events coming toward them, the boy on the
pony stunned from the photograph. I don't deny there is goodness
in this country, along with a fierce and foolish pride, and some
innocently cold determination, like those horses in Whitman's
journal stamping as they're being unsaddled. Now led three at a
time to a watering trough, the wit of their tails flicking blackflies.

MEDIEVAL WELSH POEMS

Mountain Snow

Crowcalls over mountain snow,
each field white.
No good comes of too much sleep.

Mountain snow deep on the roof,
trees bending in the wind.
Often two people love each other,
but never meet to make love.

Snow mountain air, moon full,
light in the dock-weed.
It is rare when a man makes
no claim to anything.

Stag nimble through the mountain snow.
Daring warriors are common in Britain.
It takes time to know an outsider.

Stag in rut. Mountain snow.
Ducks stringing out across a lake,
the ocean white. An old man walking
is soon overtaken.

Mountain snow. A stag searching
for something. The heart laughs at
what it loves and takes pleasure.
I have listened to many stories,
yet I never forget my disgrace.

Mountain snow. Icy-white grit.
Fish in the shallow ford.
Cave-shelter. One who acts harshly
toward another is disliked
by those watching.

A stag fleeing something. Mountain snow.
A lord swings up into his saddle,
keen swordblade close, then dismounts
with his well-armed anger. This is common.

Mountain snow. A stag with his shoulders
hunched in the cold. Many are muttering,

This is not anything like a summer day.

Stag being tracked in mountain snow.
Wind through the stone tower eaves.
Guilt weighs heavily on humanity.

Stag springing upward in mountain snow.
Wind spilling over a high white wall.
Stillness is such a beauty.

A stag surging through mountain snow.
Windsound in the roof.
What means us harm does not hide from us.

A stag on the strand, near the ocean.
Mountain snow. A man misses the way he was
when he was young. Ruined face.

Mountain snow. Stag inside a grove,
sudden raven wing, a small swift roebuck.
Someone so healthy and openhearted,
it is odd that he moans.

Mountain snow. Stag in a canebrake,
frozen marsh, mead settled in cask.
It is right for someone injured
to groan with pain.

Mountain snow. Tower speckled brown,
animals looking for cover.
It is terrible for a wife
to have an unloving husband.

Breast of a cliff splotched with lichen.
Mountain snow. Withered reedbed. The herd
turns aside from water. The sadness of a husband
whose wife is not for him a wife.

Stag in a gully. Mountain snow.
Bees deep asleep.
A thief and the long night
are perfect together.

Liverwort lobes growing
on the river surface. Mountain snow.
Someone with a sluggish mind

will not soon respond to insult.

Fish in a snow mountain lake.
Falcon aloft. A well-appointed
prince does not often sulk.

Fir-top red. Mountain snow.
Spearthrusts fierce and continuous.
Ah brothers, the longing.

A wolf loping fast along the edge
of a wilderness. Mountain snow.
Those already hurt, hurt more.

Stag attentive to the rain
falling on mountain snow. Someone sad
grows completely sullen.

Fleet deer hooves in mountain snow.
Waves soak the beach-lip.
A man conceals his purpose.

A stag in an open valley. Mountain snow.
Summer settled, lake still.
Beard-grey frost.
Brave men guard the eastern edge.

Mountain snow. Forest mottled.
My arm and shoulder are strong.
May I not live to a hundred.

Bare reedtips in mountain snow.
Fish in the depth. Top branches bent.
There is no skill without practice.

Fish in a shallow crossing-place.
Mountain snow. An old and skinny stag
is looking for a sleeping spot,
hollow like a cup, a coombe.
Longing for dead friends is a waste.

Stag in the edge of forest. Mountain snow.
The well-off do not often go on foot.
A coward brings disaster down on many.

Stag on the side hill. Mountain snow.

Wind in the ash trees.
An old man gets an extra foot, his cane.

Stag swimming the river. Mountain snow.
Ducks on the lake, the color of a lily.
Someone who won't listen is treacherous.

Red hensfeet. Mountain snow.
Creekwater making the sound it makes.
Disgrace grows larger
as you expound on it.

Nimbly moving stag. Mountain snow.
This world is not my concern.
Do not warn those already doomed.

Fleece-white snow mountain.
A friend's face so fine.
He comes again to visit.

Rooves piled white. Mountain.
If we told each other everything,
no one would live close to anyone.

Day come again. Mountain snow.
Those grieving, those half-naked
foolish people are bringing
more harm to themselves.
This is still how it is.

Redgold Chrism

Will I ever have this woman I love?
Will I enter the grove of her brightness?

Soft-silk evening star,
dragonflame in a doorway.

The Pleiades ignite their thatch-fire.
Broomstraw roan, chainmail, peacock wing.

Goldsmith, appraise this value.
Around her head in summer,
something like a slope planted
and come to graincrests tightly bound.

Peelings of birdbreast, girl-gown,
woven motion, fresh honeycomb honey,
gold cherries, watercress,
Magdalen's redgold reedbed.

Her two breasts roofed with light,
flaxen, though no plant
ever held such sun.

Chrism me as she
is christened.

A Riddle

Say who this is then.   Formed before the Flood
a powerful creature   though without flesh or bone
no nerve endings, no blood   no head, no feet

no older or younger   than when he began.
Unafraid of death   or any other terror that comes.
Cannot be put off   and never not needed.

Great God, the holy one   where did he come from
who does wonders   as great as yours?
There in the field, in the woods   moving without legs

never sick, never sad   always free of pain.
He stays the same   through all five epochs
older than   many times fifty.

Wide   as the earth's surface
he was not born   and he cannot be seen.
Unreliable   he does not come when you call.

On land and sea   absolutely necessary
unrelenting   from four directions
beyond comparison   he cannot be taught anything.

Comes out of a niche   in the sea-cliff
roaring, then hushed   he has no manners.
Savage and reckless   starting out

boisterous   loudest shouter anywhere
good and bad both   hiding
unseeable   here and there

throwing things about   with impunity.
Pays no damages   never apologizes
sometimes wet, othertimes dry.   Here he comes again.

[See Notes for answer, p. 106]

Luke Talking to his Walkingstick

Before my back got bent like this,
I had good wordcraft,
always recognized at the long table.

Before my back got bent, I was daring
and welcome in the Powys meadhall,
which is heaven for a Welshman.

Before my back got like this,
my brilliant spear was front first-piercing,
before I became this hunchback.

Wooden crook, it is fall.
Red bracken, yellow stalk.
I am through with what I love.

Bare stick, it is winter.
The men are loud into liquor.
No one comes to my bedside to talk.

Crooked wood, it is spring again.
The rosy cuckoo clears his voice.
I am unloved by any woman.

Walkingstick, it is summer.
Plowed ground has a red tinge,
with shoots curling up. I hate
the sight of your curved beak.

Walkingstick, familiar friend,
prop up this gabbling Luke.
A little more, please. Good.

Sturdy one, trusty stob.
You will be known for this work.

Age makes me look foolish. Gone the hair,
gone teeth, and the shaft that women loved.

Wind rises white in the tree fringe.
A stag stands on the rocky shield.
A frail man rouses slowly.

This dry leaf

about to break off, old,
yet born this year.

The gift so loved since I was a boy
I turn away from. The young woman,
a beautiful stranger, untried mount,
is no longer my delight.

Four things I despise descend
at once, coughing, age,
disease and grief.

I am so old. Misshapen, cold,
alone, and bent now
in three places.

Peevish, witless, boring, I whose bed
was a glory. No one visits anymore,
no women, no one, not even death
comes to call. My voice fails.

Since my sons Lew and Gawain were killed
in battle, I have grown mean, vicious.

You sorry carcass, bonestick Luke,
from the night you were born until now,
this relentless life has not let up.

Dinograd's Hunting Coat

Do you know that speckled coat
he wore when he hunted?
Speck here, here, and here.

I stitched that for him of ermine pelts.
The ermine's winter fur
is completely snow-white
with a black tip on the tail.

(a bird whistle)

I would sing out like that.
Then eight others would sound their call,
when your father started out alone
to hunt in his speckled coat.

Spear across his shoulder, finishing club
in the right hand, calling his hounds,

Giff, Gaff, sic, sic, seek'm, fetch,
fetch, sic'm, sic, Gaff, Giff.

He could spearfish from the bow
of a coracle as easy as a mountain lion
bats a small animal, touching
the water almost gently.

When your father went further afield
in winter deep into the mountains,
he always came back with game:

stag, the dwarf deer we call roe, grouse,
fish from the pool at Derwennydd Falls,
nothing ever got away from the point
of that lance he threw, wild boar, fox, lynx,
unless, of course, it happened to have wings!

Central Asian Sufis And The Nature Of The Heart

Central Asian Sufis
and the Nature of the Heart

Yasavi makes his living in Bokhara
carving wooden spoons, smoothsanded,
superbly curved spoons.

To hold one in both hands
is to become a lover of the world again,
and of how beauty can enter into form
through craftsmanship,
in case you have forgotten
how that goes, as daily we do.

Yasavi has an ox
that walks alone around town
carrying the spoons in a saddlebag.
Possible customers come up. It stops,
while they reach in and pull out spoons,
find the one they want,
then put the others back in the bag
with a payment of money or barter.

If someone does not pay, or pays wrongly,
the ox follows him through the market,
into his house, to the mosque, wherever he goes
until the transaction is made right.

The ox is fair,
and supremely stubborn.

Oxen in their front-facing
see more than you might think.

With evening prayer
the ox returns to Yasavi,
who collects the takings, and tends
to the simple needs, water,
hay, a bedding spot.

They wake to the next day's spoonwork,
and the wandering among market-walkers,
who have no idea how much
they are about to want a shallow spoon

made of ash or oak, or a ladle of cypress.

Imaginal scenes come to the customers
as they stand beside the ox
holding an implement
for tasting soup.

A gathering of friends,
a merging of candles in firstdark,
events yet to happen.

It is as it was before
the wideopen spill and stir
of the great tureen of galaxies.

We want the daily dissolving into work
that Yasavi and his ox have.

****

Husam al-Balkhi devises a way
to spend his days and nights.

Available to visitors
from early morning to afternoon prayer,
he talks with whoever comes,
laughs and tells stories.

Then late afternoon through the night
he is completely alone, responds to no
questions. He does not speak again
until the sun rises the next day.

It is good to have a record
of experiments others have made
dividing their time between
conversation and solitude.

They help us to try new ways,
in spite of the botheration
it is for those around us.

Balkh, where Husam lived, is a ruin,
or less than a ruin, a raised circle
a mile and a half across, with a rounded
berm, a brim where the wall was.

In the bowl of Balkh are sheep grazing
and paths. No structure or any sign of one.

All that will eventually go away
has gone away in Balkh.

They say it took ninety camels
to carry the books Bahauddin, Rumi's father,
took when he left in 1220 ahead
of the disaster arriving on Mongolian horses.

I am nostalgic for some way
I have never been.

I used to be more given to trance,
more rapt. The writing impulses now
come more from turning on myself
to face weakness, the float,
or from finding a wandering way
that invites language along with it.

****

Jami explains his pen-name with a pun.
Jam is the town he was born in.
Jam means cup.

My pen writes with what drips
from the cup of surrender.

Here is how he met
his teacher, Kashghari.

In his late teens Jami's path through Herat
took him everyday by where Kashghari
was talking with students.

Kashghari would think, This is
a very talented young man. He has captivated
my heart, but I do not know how to catch him.

Jami becomes infatuated with a young woman,
and in order to rid himself of the obsession,
he leaves Herat and goes to Samarcand.

Kashghari appears to him there in a dream,

saying, *Come, brother. Find a loved one
you can never leave.*

Moved by the dream, Jami
returns to Herat and is initiated
by Kashghari, who says,

To reach God is much easier
than to succeed on the material plane,
where one must always look
for something before finding it.

In the case of the divine mystery,
you have to already be inside it
before you feel inclined to look.

****

Jami does not take students.
He feels daunted by the prospect
of guiding another person's soulgrowth.

Here are lines from his poetry.

> I look for you everywhere
> when you *are* that everywhere.
> I am a fool.

> You are concealed
> in how you are revealed.
> I am a fool.

> I turn the pages of the book
> of the universe. I see only
> the oceanic mystery that stays the same,
> though always changing, never the same,
> always the same, and I am a fool.

> If I were to speak the great secrets
> of consciousness, what would I use? Words?

> The spell must be broken,
> or we will never reach.

> Existence is an enchantment
> where we think in terms of inner and outer.

Peaceful mind, painful body.
Resting body, passionate mind.
Both can be transcended.

There is a nook inside nowhere,
where your love and my love live,
have lived. The wine of this friendship
circulated in my blood
before any grapevine spread root-fingers
out looking for water to alchemize.

****

Sayyid Hasan, still a small boy,
is taken to see Ubaidallah.

A dish of honey is there.
He begins taking tastes
with his finger.

The Sufi teacher asks his name.
He looks up and says, *Honey.*

This tickles the teacher so
he takes the child as his student,
admiring the boy's capacity
for total immersion in the thing he loves.

****

Ubahi leaves his conventional college
in Samarcand. He has fallen in love with Sufism.
He sets out for Kuh-i Nur, the mountain of light,
where a great teacher is in meditation.

The road to the mountain
leads by Ubaidallah's school.

Ubahi walking, sees the teacher ride up
and dismount by the gate. He decides
to postpone his journey until he has met this man.

He walks into the school and sits with the group
facing the teacher, whose head is bowed.

Ubaidallah raises his head

and recites two lines of poetry.

> The mountain is no longer a refuge.
> It is better to stay with me.

Ubahi thinks, If this teacher
has spoken these lines for me,
let him repeat them.

Ubaidallah turns his head and says the lines
directly to Ubahi, addressing him by name.
Then he gets up, mounts his horse, and rides away.

Ubahi feels dazed and confused.
Later he joins Ubaidallah's school
and spends thirty years in his presence.

Ubahi says of the soul's motion,

> Enjoy the state you are in,
> and never quit longing
> or those to come.

> What you have now is a drop
> compared to the ocean
> that will cover you later.

I want to be more
in the company of those
who feel the soul's motion around
them and moving them around.

Ubaidallah:

> Close the door of teaching,
> and open the door of friendship.

> Close the door of solitude.
> Open the door of companionship.

****

My conversation with Naqshaband.

> I do not know
> the true nature of the heart,
> but someone has told me

it is like the moon
when it is three days old.

Naqshaband is standing close.
He puts his right foot on my left.

An exultation fills me.
I see the whole universe inside myself.
When I return to my ordinary state,
Naqshaband says, That is the heart.

You cannot know what it is
until you feel the extent,
the capaciousness.

What you have just seen
is how one knows the heart.

****

Naqshaband and I are doing stone
and mortar work. Others are helping.

At noon he calls a break.
Each finds a shady place to sleep.
My spot leaves my muddy feet
out in the sun.

As we sleep Bahauddin Naqshaband
walks among us seeing
how we sleep.

When he comes to me, he kneels
and puts his cheek against
my sundrying mudfeet.

Says, have mercy
on these feet.

I sleep well
into the afternoon.

These old ones
are how the soul
would love to live.

And how is that? Generously,

with clear honesty, in some
sinfully wild makingness.
There is no telling.

****

The heart represents
the attainment of annihilation.

The *sound* heart is a condition
of direct vision that comes
to masters of permanent non-existence,
the stage of complete annihilation.

The heart is also called
the comprehensive human reality.

The language here is latinate
and theological, distancing us
from what is either
our central experience, or fantasy.

But for some reason this diction
brings in a mysterious *mental* dimension
to heart that helps me know
the breadth of its field.

****

Najmuddin Kubra is standing
in a doorway. A dog trots by.
Their eyes meet.

The condition of the dog changes.
He loses himself and now
wherever he goes, other dogs gather.

Each comes and puts its paws
on the paws of the surrendered dog,
then withdraws a respectful distance.

****

Yasavi, the oxman
spoonmaker, says:

I drink the wine of unity
and fall inside the glass.

The emptiness there is full.
Four hundred thousand wise men
and women are circling.

I walk among them asking
the object of my search.

To my amazement they all say,
It is within you.

The universe is an empty
wine jar. We drank
the wine. We did.

Now we circle inside the empty jar
like pilgrims on hajj arrived at the kaaba,
going round the kaaba, asking
where is it, where is it,
being told, inside you, inside you.

****

Shams Tabriz says
if the kaaba were suddenly lifted up
out of this world, we would see
that in five-times prayer
each of us is bowing to the other,
everyone to every other.

No need for forms of worship.
Take religion out of the picture.
Let friendship be openly
what it already is.

****

The scrapwood man in Shiraz
has a onefoot square, makeshift table
that he saws larger pieces
into kindling on with a hacksaw.

He looks up at us as we pass,

puts the table and the saw aside,
and holds out both arms
to us, smiling.

No language. He has no words
from any word-lineage anymore.

He gestures toward a bulletin board
of pictures, photos of himself
in younger years, very alive and charismatic.
He looks like the young Meher Baba.

Irregular woodfruit pieces
hang about the shallow storefront.

We stop and put our hands
across our chests and bow,
but we do not stay.

We could have sat down
and let him show us how to accept
unwanted wood from neighbors,
how to cut it to a proper length,
then bind those into bundles for the fires
that people on this street
are apt to make.

So it continues as a grief
and a brightening mistake,
that I often do not forsake
the habitual to accept the company
of the scrapwood man's eyes.

                    ****

Another refusal, a continuing on
that is a turning away,
not from wordless conversation,
but from brave talking.

This with the grace I am given
time to be in the presence of,
Bawa Muhaiyaddeen.

Early in those nine years,

maybe on the second *day,*

I was leaving, going to the airport,
back home, on the landing
coming down from the upstairs bedroom
where he received visitors and talked,
sitting crosslegged on his bed.

He came to the top railing and called.
Did I want to have some private time
with him? I waved the opportunity
away, saying I'll be coming back.

Is it fear of meeting the nakedest core,
the one who knows all my secrets,
where they lead, where they came from?

I never brought it up, talking with him
afterward. The denial was such,
I just *now* remember it.

I want to go back, still frightened
by the scalding, icy springwater,
up that half-flight of stairs.

I have skirted the edge
of disintegration, edge
of union, on the teasing curl
of something evermore about to be,
as Wordsworth said of April.
Close, but no *fana.*

I see the failure of courage,
failure to be fully alive,
my characteristic failure,
not to respond with full spontaneity,
generosity, fearless imagination,
openhearted confession, whatever
consciousness I might muster,
without holding back.

I have often avoided
the wholehearted *yes,*
saying there is plenty
of time. There is not.

Think about it some. Take it easy.
That is the continuous advice
of the cowardly *nafs*,
that want things *not* to change.

What I want is the moment
on the landing again.

Best quit wanting
a wistful impossibility.
Accept the friendship I have.

I was riding in a car in Minneapolis
last November with a nun, Irene O'Neill,
who told me that a spirit-seeing woman
saw a small dark man with me
during my reading at Pax Christi.
Then she saw he was inside me.

I wonder what is true.
Let me not move away
too quickly ever again
from the scrapwood man.

****

Naqshaband met a wanderer one day
in the big square of Bokhara.

Where are you from?

I have no idea.

Where are you going?

I have no plan.

What is goodness?

No idea.

What is evil?

Hands-up, who-knows gesture.

How do you determine right behavior?

Whatever is good for me.

And bad, I suppose, is whatever
seems unhelpful for yourself?

Yes.

The crowd that has gathered around this conversation
grows irritated with the non-answers
of the wanderer. They push him away,
so they can speak more substantively
with their master Naqshaband.

The man goes striding off
in a direction where there is no town
or anything, as far as anyone knows.

Fools, says Naqshaband.

This man is showing you
what your behavior looks like.

It is a truth we do not know
where we came from or where we are going,
what good and bad consist of,
or which direction in the present moment
we should choose to follow next.

****

There is a swordsmith
in a valley in eastern Afghanistan.

When there is no war, he forges
steel ploughs, and he shoes horses,
but he is most known for his singing.

People come from all over to listen to him,
from the forests of the giant walnut trees,
from Qataghan and Badakshan,
from the snowbound Hindu Kush,
from Khanabad and Kunat,
from Herat and Paghman.

Mostly they come to hear one song
about the far valley of paradise.

This particular song has a haunting lilt

and the ability to make those who hear
feel that they are in that place,
the paradisal valley.

Someone always asks when he finishes,
Is that a real place?

It is as real as real can be,
is always his answer.

Have you been there?

Not in the ordinary way of traveling.

The singer loves Aisha,
a young woman in the valley.

But she doubts that there is
such a place as the one he sings of,
and so does his rival for her love,
Hasan, a swordsman of great strength
and agility. He has full confidence
that he will eventually win Aisha.

He makes fun of the swordsmith-singer
whenever he can. One day the villagers
are sitting inside the blessed quiet
that happens after that song.

Hasan says, Why don't you follow
the blue haze that rises there
from the mountains of Sangan,
and actually *go* to the place you sing about?

I feel it would not be right.

Well, that is a convenient feeling.
It keeps you from being revealed
as a fraud and a sentimental dreamer.

I propose a test to decide
several things at once.

You love Aisha,
but she does not believe
in your valley.

You two could never be married
in such a discord of trust.

You expect me then
to set out for the valley and return
with proof of its existence?

Yes! call out Hasan
and the crowd together.

I will make this trip then,
but will Aisha promise to marry me
if I return successfully?

I will, says Aisha quietly.

He collects dried mulberries
and scraps of bread in a sack
and starts on the journey.

His way is always up. He climbs
until he comes to a sheer wall
blocking the way. He scales that,
and there is another, another,
five walls in all.

On the other side of the last wall
he finds himself in a valley
like his own.

People come out of their houses
to welcome him.

It is so weirdly strange, this experience
of the swordsmith-singer.

Months later he walks back into
the valley he started out from,
an old man limping to his hut.

Word spreads that he has returned.
Hasan is spokesman for the crowd that comes.
He calls the singer to the window.

They gasp at how old he has become.

Did you find the valley?

I did.

What was it like?

He is quiet for a while
in the weariness and confusion,
in the difficulty of saying
where he went, where he is now,
and what has happened.

I climbed until it seemed like
no human habitation could be so high.
But there was, a valley identical to this one.

And the people there are not only *like*
us, they *are* us. Hasan, Aisha, myself,
you, you, everyone is there
in his or her original form.

We are the shadowy copies.

Everyone turns and walks away,
convinced that the singer has gone mad
in his solitary search.

Aisha marries Hasan.
The singer rapidly grows old and dies.

The people who heard the story
as he told it also grow soon old.
They lose interest in their lives.

They feel some huge event is about to occur,
one they have no control over.
Vital energy drains away.

Once in a thousand years
such a secret is revealed
to someone like the singer-swordsmith.

But no one yet
has been able to take in quite
the truth that we are two selves,
this one and one more real,
that lives in the valley
a certain song makes us long for.

That we are that being
as well as this more familiar one,
who is dubious, confused, reckless, and sad,
whose sadness is a little solved
when we hear the song
that makes us remember essence.

A friend says,
There *is* another world,
and this is it.

That the two valleys are one
living-being
cannot be said in language.

That we already *are* the perfected one
cannot be spoken of.

But it can be *felt* inside,
as the moment itself,

and as the whole outdoors,
the whole-around-us,
that veiny animule.

That is the heart,
where we take our walks.

****

Three lines from Ansari.

> A voice whispers to me in the night,
> There is no such thing
> as a voice that whispers in the night.

****

An old dervish tavern song.

> It may be *said,* They came here in vain,
> but let it not *be* they came here in vain.

> We leave this to you, this that can be left.
> We worked on it as much as we could.
> We leave the rest for you to finish.

Remember, you are trusted
with this work. And remember,
my friend, we will meet again.

NOTES

Wine Poems—The book I was reading that night was *Selected Poems, Po Chu-i,* translated by Burton Watson, Columbia University Press (New York, 2000), pages 66, 68, 65, and others.

Gurdjieff's Teaching—This story is retold from Fritz Peters' *Boyhood with Gurdjieff,* Capra Press (Santa Barbara, 1980), pp.49-51.

Purring—This poem appeared in an earlier collection, *Tentmaking* (2002), with different lineation.

The Sound Made by Snapping the Fingers—In the spring of 1968, at thirty-one, I wrote a sequence of short, haikuesque Body Poems. This poem is a garrulous continuation, at seventy, of that series.

Just This Once—This was first spoken on March 15, 2003 in the National Cathedral in Washington a few days before the American invasion of Iraq.

American College Students Overheard in a Restaurant After I Have Returned from Afghanistan—In March 2005 the U.S.State Department sent me as the first speaker to Afghanistan in twenty-five years. *Stormy* is someone's nickname. *Cloudy* was my nickname in college.

Stern Mystics and Secret Governmental Murder—*Unio Mystica* was published by Osho International, 1980. The second edition, with this introduction was published in 2003. Copies may be ordered from Maypop Books (800-682-8637) or from the website, *colemanbarks.com. The Time Needed*—This Hakim Sanai (1044-1150) poem is reworked from an E. G. Browne translation.

Soulmaking and the Coming Bomb—*The Peace Tax Fund* is sponsored by The National Campaign for a Peace Tax Fund. They may be contacted at info@peacetaxfund.org or at 2121 Decatur Place NW, Washington, DC 20008. *Jonathan Granoff* is an attorney and international peace activist. He is dedicated to the total elimination of nuclear weapons. He is current president of the Global Security Institute and vice-president of the NGO Committee on Disarmament, Peace, and Security at the UN. Jonathan is a good friend, and not so susceptible as I am to the *boredom* of peacemaking, or if he is, he dismisses it as beside-the-point, and luxurious. Get on with the work. Right. But there is such a powerful narcotic built in to the process, for those of us who are trying to find an alternative to war. The tendency to nod off is always a clear and present danger. I feel we should acknowledge that and do what we can with humor and whatever nutso ideas might keep us alert.

Mountain Snow—Joseph Clancy says this poem has *radial* form, meaning it has no beginning, middle, or end, but rather is all center, a hub with its thirty-six stanza-spokes. Each stanza begins by mentioning mountain snow and some solitary animal in motion, sometimes in danger, a stag, a falcon. Windsound comes in, reedbeds, liverwort globes floating on a river, a white wall, a tower. The outdoor scene is honored. Then comes a blunt comment on the human predicament, a turn indoors if you will. Sometimes wrenching, sometimes light and gnomic. These abrupt statements conclude each winter, haikuesque, Brueghalesque, scene. I hear in the form an elder poetry, a setting for the contemplation and conversation in a circle of elders, with much music and silence between stanzas. All medieval Welsh poetry was accompanied by music. Inside this contemplative center various truths about aggression and betrayal are examined, as well the many forms of sadness and desperation. I hear in the core of the poem the wise emptiness found in true elders, the depth of old blue singers and jazz musicians. Joseph Clancy, *Medieval Welsh Poems,* pp.111-114, Four Courts Press (Dublin, Ireland and Portland, OR, 2003).

Redgold Chrism—By Dafydd ab Edmund (fl. 1450-1495), a poet known mostly for his love poems, and for how he transformed Welsh poetry at the Carmathen eisteddfod in 1453. With his performance at that yearly event he significantly increased the level of difficulties a bard needed to master. Clancy calls this poem "A Girl's Hair," pp.329-330. *Chrism* refers to a consecrated annointing oil mixed with balm, and it is also the name of the child's pure-white robe worn at christening.

A Riddle—Anonymous, from the 10th century. This is the only surviving riddle poem in medieval Welsh. There are several in Anglo-Saxon. *The wind* is the answer not given in the poem, but in Clancy's notes. Another answer might be inspiration, the creative invigorating presence, what Sufis call *the friend,* the surprise barrel-though that moves among us, as it pleases. Inspiration and wind have always informed one another. Clancy, pp.114-115.

The *five epochs* in medieval thought are (1) From the Creation to the Flood. (2) From the Flood to Abraham. (3) From Abraham to David. (4) From David to Israel's captivity. (5) From Moses to Jesus. The sixth is the one we live now, from Christ until Doomsday.

Many times fifty—Fifty being the age when one was considered old, in the 10th century.

Luke Talking to his Walkingstick—By an unknown poet in the 9th century. The speaker, Llywarch, whom I call Luke, is a 6th century figure known from other poems as an old man who urges his several sons (twenty-one of them!) to go into battle as he had gone. He loses them one after the other in the attempt to defend Powys, northeastern Wales, from Briton invaders. In Clancy's anthology the poem is called "Complaint in Old Age," pp.87-89.

Llywarch's conversation with his stick-figure stage-prop companion is familiar to us. Lear in his rant, Hamlet with Yorick's skull. Jack Nicholson in almost anything, E.A.Robinson's Eben Flood ("Mr.Flood's Party") out in the moonlight somewhere between tavern and home, Beckett's anti-hero in fine fettle on the dump. Conversation and self-conversation are deep human delights, and a ground of being. Luke is one of the early literary practitioners. Our national American poets, Walt Whitman and Emily Dickinson, work in this region. *I stop somewhere waiting for you*, says Whitman at the end of "Song of Myself." Emily Dickinson is continually addressing and invoking a *shapeless friend*, an intuition of *company, presence* (#773).

Dinograd's Hunting Coat—From about 650 CE. This anonymous poem was copied by a scribe into the manuscript of *The Gododdin*, a battle poem, as marginalia. It may well be spoken in a woman's voice, by the boy's mother. The speaker is the one who has sewn the jacket. If the poem is written by a woman, it is the oldest we have from the British Isles. The poem is a moving elegy sung or spoken for the child, a remembering of his father's hunting skills. In the loving joke at the end, I hear how close the woman is to her son, and to the boy's dead father too. A scholar has located Derwynnydd Falls as a spot called Lodore Force, which flows into Derwentwater in Cumbria, north of Wales. Clancy calls this, "Song for a Small Boy," p.97.

Central Asian Sufis and the Nature of the Heart—Told and retold, such incidents come down in the oral tradition. Hasan Shushud put them in *Masters of Wisdom of Central Asia,* published in Turkish as *Hecegan Hanedani* (1958) and translated into English by Muhtar Holland and published by Coombe Springs Press in 1983.

Ahmed Yasavi (1046-1166)
Najmuddin Kubra (died 1221)
Bahauddin Naqshaband (1318-1389)
Ubaidallah Ahrar (1404-1490)

Birth and death dates are not known for Husam al-Balkhi, Sayyid Hasan, or Abu Sa'id Ubahi, who were friends and students of Ubaidallah, or for Sa'd al-Din Kashghari, Jami's teacher. All were alive in the fifteenth century.

Mevlana Jami (1414-1492).

The singer-swordsmith story—This is retold from Idries Shah's *The Wisdom of the Idiots,* as are the story of the wanderer Naqshband meets in the Bokhara market, the lines from Ansari (1006-1089), and the dervish tavern song.

Naqshaband is known for his love of craftsmanship. Near the tomb of Ansari in Herat is a block of marble carved like layers of lace. Deep inside itself the cave-levels of carving continue, the ultimate craftsmanship mystery, inexplicable, immoveable. The Russians tried to take it with them to Moscow when they left Afghanistan, but they could not. There is a stone dog in front of the Ansari tomb area, beautifully smoothed by hands that have loved how he loves his master.